The
GREAT YANKEE COVERUP

∼ THE LOCHLAINN SEABROOK COLLECTION ∼

Everything You Were Taught About the Civil War is Wrong, Ask a Southerner!
Everything You Were Taught About American Slavery is Wrong, Ask a Southerner!
Give This Book to a Yankee! A Southern Guide to the Civil War For Northerners
Honest Jeff and Dishonest Abe: A Southern Children's Guide to the Civil War
Confederacy 101: Amazing Facts You Never Knew About America's Oldest Political Tradition
Slavery 101: Amazing Facts You Never Knew About America's "Peculiar Institution"
The Great Yankee Coverup: What the North Doesn't Want You to Know About Lincoln's War!
Confederate Blood and Treasure: An Interview With Lochlainn Seabrook
Confederate Flag Facts: What Every American Should Know About Dixie's Southern Cross
A Rebel Born: A Defense of Nathan Bedford Forrest - Confederate General, American Legend (winner of the 2011 Jefferson Davis Historical Gold Medal)
A Rebel Born: The Screenplay
Nathan Bedford Forrest: Southern Hero, American Patriot - Honoring a Confederate Icon and the Old South
The Quotable Nathan Bedford Forrest: Selections From the Writings and Speeches of the Confederacy's Most Brilliant Cavalryman
Give 'Em Hell Boys! The Complete Military Correspondence of Nathan Bedford Forrest
Forrest! 99 Reasons to Love Nathan Bedford Forrest
Saddle, Sword, and Gun: A Biography of Nathan Bedford Forrest For Teens
Nathan Bedford Forrest and the Battle of Fort Pillow: Yankee Myth, Confederate Fact
Nathan Bedford Forrest and the Ku Klux Klan: Yankee Myth, Confederate Fact
The Quotable Jefferson Davis: Selections From the Writings and Speeches of the Confederacy's First President
The Quotable Alexander H. Stephens: Selections From the Writings and Speeches of the Confederacy's First Vice President
The Alexander H. Stephens Reader: Excerpts From the Works of a Confederate Founding Father
The Quotable Robert E. Lee: Selections From the Writings and Speeches of the South's Most Beloved Civil War General
The Old Rebel: Robert E. Lee As He Was Seen By His Contemporaries
The Articles of Confederation Explained: A Clause-by-Clause Study of America's First Constitution
The Constitution of the Confederate States of America Explained: A Clause-by-Clause Study of the South's Magna Carta
The Quotable Stonewall Jackson: Selections From the Writings and Speeches of the South's Most Famous General
Abraham Lincoln: The Southern View - Demythologizing America's Sixteenth President
The Unquotable Abraham Lincoln: The President's Quotes They Don't Want You To Know!
Lincolnology: The Real Abraham Lincoln Revealed in His Own Words - A Study of Lincoln's Suppressed, Misinterpreted, and Forgotten Writings and Speeches
The Great Impersonator! 99 Reasons to Dislike Abraham Lincoln
The Quotable Edward A. Pollard: Selections From the Writings of the Confederacy's Greatest Defender
Encyclopedia of the Battle of Franklin - A Comprehensive Guide to the Conflict that Changed the Civil War
Carnton Plantation Ghost Stories: True Tales of the Unexplained from Tennessee's Most Haunted Civil War House!
The McGavocks of Carnton Plantation: A Southern History - Celebrating One of Dixie's Most Noble Confederate Families and Their Tennessee Home
Jesus and the Law of Attraction: The Bible-Based Guide to Creating Perfect Health, Wealth, and Happiness Following Christ's Simple Formula
The Bible and the Law of Attraction: 99 Teachings of Jesus, the Apostles, and the Prophets
Christ Is All and In All: Rediscovering Your Divine Nature and the Kingdom Within
Jesus and the Gospel of Q: Christ's Pre-Christian Teachings As Recorded in the New Testament
Seabrook's Bible Dictionary of Traditional and Mystical Christian Doctrines
The Way of Holiness: The Story of Religion and Myth From the Cave Bear Cult to Christianity
Christmas Before Christianity: How the Birthday of the "Sun" Became the Birthday of the "Son"
Britannia Rules: Goddess-Worship in Ancient Anglo-Celtic Society - An Academic Look at the United Kingdom's Matricentric Spiritual Past
The Book of Kelle: An Introduction to Goddess-Worship and the Great Celtic Mother-Goddess Kelle, Original Blessed Lady of Ireland
The Goddess Dictionary of Words and Phrases: Introducing a New Core Vocabulary for the Women's Spirituality Movement
Princess Diana: Modern Day Moon-Goddess - A Psychoanalytical and Mythological Look at Diana Spencer's Life, Marriage, and Death (with Dr. Jane Goldberg)
Aphrodite's Trade: The Hidden History of Prostitution Unveiled
UFOs and Aliens: The Complete Guidebook
The Caudills: An Etymological, Ethnological, and Genealogical Study - Exploring the Name and National Origins of a European-American Family
The Blakeneys: An Etymological, Ethnological, and Genealogical Study - Uncovering the Mysterious Origins of the Blakeney Family and Name

Five-Star Books & Gifts With Five-Star Service!

SeaRavenPress.com

The GREAT YANKEE COVERUP

What the North Doesn't Want You to Know About Lincoln's War!

Lochlainn Seabrook

JEFFERSON DAVIS HISTORICAL GOLD MEDAL WINNER

FOREWORD BY THOMAS V. STRAIN JR.

ILLUSTRATED

Sea Raven Press, Nashville, Tennessee, USA

THE GREAT YANKEE COVERUP

Published by
Sea Raven Press, Cassidy Ravensdale, President
PO Box 1484, Spring Hill, Tennessee 37174-1484 USA
SeaRavenPress.com • searavenpress@gmail.com

Copyright © 2015 Lochlainn Seabrook
in accordance with U.S. and international copyright laws and regulations, as stated and protected under the Berne Union for the Protection of Literary and Artistic Property (Berne Convention), and the Universal Copyright Convention (the UCC). All rights reserved under the Pan-American and International Copyright Conventions.

1st paperback edition, 1st printing: June 2015 • 1st paperback edition, 2nd printing: August 2015
1st hardcover edition (978-1-943737-06-2): August 2015

ISBN: 978-0-9913779-8-5 (paperback)
Library of Congress Control Number: 2015939609

This work is the copyrighted intellectual property of Lochlainn Seabrook and has been registered with the Copyright Office at the Library of Congress in Washington, D.C., USA. No part of this work (including text, covers, drawings, photos, illustrations, maps, images, diagrams, etc.), in whole or in part, may be used, reproduced, stored in a retrieval system, or transmitted, in any form or by any means now known or hereafter invented, without written permission from the publisher. The sale, duplication, hire, lending, copying, digitalization, or reproduction of this material, in any manner or form whatsoever, is also prohibited, and is a violation of federal, civil, and digital copyright law, which provides severe civil and criminal penalties for any violations.

The Great Yankee Coverup: What the North Doesn't Want You to Know About Lincoln's War!, by Lochlainn Seabrook. Foreword by Thomas V. Strain Jr. Includes an index, endnotes, and bibliographical references.

Front and back cover design and art, book design, layout, and interior art by Lochlainn Seabrook
Typography: Sea Raven Press Book Design
All images, graphic design, graphic art, and illustrations copyright © Lochlainn Seabrook
Cover image & design: "The Confederate Triumvirate," copyright © by Lochlainn Seabrook
Portions of this book have been adapted from the author's other works

The views on the American "Civil War" documented in this book are those of the publisher.

Dedication

To Southern women, past, present, and future.
You are the foundation of Dixie.

6 ~ The Great Yankee Coverup

Epigraph

"Everyone should do all in his power to collect and disseminate the truth."

Robert E. Lee
December 3, 1865

CONTENTS

Notes to the Reader - 9
Foreword, by Thomas V. Strain Jr. - 11
Introduction, by Lochlainn Seabrook - 15

SECTION ONE
POLITICS & SECESSION

Fact 1 - 27
Fact 2 - 31
Fact 3 - 33
Fact 4 - 35
Fact 5 - 36
Fact 6 - 39
Fact 7 - 41
Fact 8 - 42
Fact 9 - 43
Fact 10 - 44
Fact 11   46
Fact 12 - 47

SECTION TWO
LINCOLN'S WAR

Fact 13 - 51
Fact 14 - 55
Fact 15 - 56
Fact 16 - 59
Fact 17 - 62
Fact 18 - 63
Fact 19 - 66
Fact 20 - 67
Fact 21 - 68
Fact 22 - 69
Fact 23 - 72
Fact 24 - 74
Fact 25 - 76
Fact 26 - 77
Fact 27 - 78
Fact 28 - 79
Fact 29 - 80

SECTION THREE
RACE & SLAVERY

Fact 30 - 86
Fact 31 - 87
Fact 32 - 89
Fact 33 - 91
Fact 34 - 92
Fact 35 - 93
Fact 36 - 95
Fact 37 - 96
Fact 38 - 97
Fact 39 - 99
Fact 40 - 101
Fact 41 - 102
Fact 42 - 103
Fact 43 - 104

Fact 44 - 106
Fact 45 - 107
Fact 46 - 108
Fact 47 - 109
Fact 48 - 110
Fact 49 - 111
Fact 50 - 113
Fact 51 - 114
Fact 52 - 115
Fact 53 - 116
Fact 54 - 117
Fact 55 - 118
Fact 56 - 119
Fact 57 - 120
Fact 58 - 122
Fact 59 - 123
Fact 60 - 124
Fact 61 - 125
Fact 62 - 126
Fact 63 - 128
Fact 64 - 129

Fact 65 - 130
Fact 66 - 132
Fact 67 - 134
Fact 68 - 135
Fact 69 - 137
Fact 70 - 138
Fact 71 - 140
Fact 72 - 142
Fact 73 - 144
Fact 74 - 146
Fact 75 - 147
Fact 76 - 149
Fact 77 - 150
Fact 78 - 151
Fact 79 - 152
Fact 80 - 153
Fact 81 - 154
Fact 82 - 156
Fact 83 - 157
Fact 84 - 158
Fact 85 - 159

SECTION FOUR
DAVIS & LINCOLN

Fact 86 - 162
Fact 87 - 164
Fact 88 - 165
Fact 89 - 167
Fact 90 - 168
Fact 91 - 170
Fact 92 - 173

Fact 93 - 181
Fact 94 - 182
Fact 95 - 183
Fact 96 - 186
Fact 97 - 188
Fact 98 - 189
Fact 99 - 190

Notes - 195
Bibliography - 198
Index - 199
Meet the Author - 206
Meet the Foreword Writer - 208

NOTES TO THE READER

☛ In any study of America's antebellum, bellum, and postbellum periods, it is vitally important to understand that in 1860 the two major political parties—the Democrats and the newly formed Republicans—were the opposite of what they are today. In other words, the Democrats of the mid 19th Century were Conservatives, akin to the Republican Party of today, while the Republicans of the mid 19th Century were Liberals, akin to the Democratic Party of today.

Thus the Confederacy's Democratic president, Jefferson Davis, was a Conservative (with libertarian leanings); the Union's Republican president, Abraham Lincoln, was a Liberal (with socialistic leanings). This is why, in the mid 1800s, the conservative wing of the Democratic Party was known as "the States' Rights Party."[1]

Hence, the Democrats of the Civil War period referred to themselves as "conservatives," "confederates," "anti-centralists," or "constitutionalists" (the latter because they favored strict adherence to the original Constitution—which tacitly guaranteed states' rights—as created by the Founding Fathers), while the Republicans called themselves "liberals," "nationalists," "centralists," or "consolidationists" (the latter three because they wanted to nationalize the central government and consolidate political power in Washington, D.C.).[2]

The author's cousin, Confederate Vice President and Democrat Alexander H. Stephens: a Southern Conservative.

Since this idea is new to most of my readers, let us further demystify it by viewing it from the perspective of the American Revolutionary War. If Davis and his conservative Southern constituents (the Democrats of 1861) had been alive in 1775, they would have sided with George Washington and the American colonists, who sought to secede from the tyrannical government of Great Britain; if Lincoln and his Liberal Northern constituents (the Republicans of 1861) had been alive at that time, they would have sided with King George III and the English monarchy, who sought to maintain the American colonies as possessions of the British Empire. It is due to this very comparison that Southerners often refer to the "Civil War" as the Second American Revolutionary War.

10 ∽ THE GREAT YANKEE COVERUP

☞ As I heartily dislike the phrase "Civil War," its use throughout this book (as well as in my other works) is worthy of an explanation.

Today America's entire literary system refers to the conflict of 1861 using the Northern term the "Civil War," whether we in the South like it or not. Thus, as all book searches by readers, libraries, and retail outlets are now performed online, and as all bookstores categorize works from this period under the heading "Civil War," book publishers and authors who deal with this particular topic have little choice but to use this term themselves. If I were to refuse to use it, as some of my Southern colleagues have suggested, few people would ever find or read my books.

Add to this the fact that scarcely any non-Southerners have ever heard of the names we in the South use for the conflict, such as the "War for Southern Independence"—or my personal preference, "Lincoln's War." It only makes sense then to use the term "Civil War" in most commercial situations.

We should also bear in mind that while today educated persons, particularly educated Southerners, all share an abhorrence for the phrase "Civil War," it was not always so. Confederates who lived through and even fought in the conflict regularly used the term throughout the 1860s, and even long after. Among them were Confederate generals such as Nathan Bedford Forrest, Richard Taylor, and Joseph E. Johnston, not to mention the Confederacy's vice president, Alexander H. Stephens. Even the Confederacy's highest leader, President Jefferson Davis, used the term "Civil War,"[3] and in one case at least, as late as 1881—the year he wrote his brilliant exposition, *The Rise and Fall of the Confederate Government*.[4]

☞ The title of this book is not meant to be an indictment of *all* Yankees. Some of the strongest supporters of the South are from the Northern states (known as "Copperheads"), while some of the South's severest critics are from Dixie (known as "scallywags"). Rather the focus of this work is on the anti-South propaganda machine that has its roots in the Old North, and its biased, conformist, provincial, unenlightened, South-hating 18th- and 19th-Century Yankee creators. The modern day descendants of this group remain the principle instigators and disseminators of The Great Yankee Coverup, and it is they to whom the title refers.

☞ Lincoln's War on the American people and the Constitution can ever be fully understood without a thorough knowledge of the South's perspective. As *The Great Yankee Coverup* is only meant to be a brief introductory guide to these topics, one cannot hope to learn the whole truth about them here. For those who are interested in a more in-depth study, please see my other more scholarly books, listed on page 2; in particular, my title, *Everything You Were Taught About the Civil War is Wrong, Ask a Southerner!*

FOREWORD

One of the most misunderstood and purposefully misrepresented times in the history of the United States is the period leading up to and including the invasion of the South in what ultimately resulted in the War Between the States. To truly understand the actual causes of the War one has to go and research the years and decades prior to the firing on Fort Sumter on April 12, 1861, and to gain some understanding of the nature of the "union" and its original design.

Rejecting the "Virginia Plan" in 1788 at the Philadelphia Convention, a plan which called for a strong "national" government, our Colonial forefathers opted instead for a "Confederation" of States—a compact among individual "States" which reserved to themselves all powers not expressly delegated to the "general" government within the constitution.

Less than 75 years later, when the South attempted to withdraw from this "compact", withdrawal or "secession" being a power "reserved to the States, they were subsequently invaded by the North. What prompted this invasion? Simply put, it was the unilateral actions of a tyrannical would-be monarch named Abraham Lincoln who, rejecting the "compact" theory upon which the federation had been founded, regarded "preserving the union" to be more important than the right of the States to self-government. One of our venerable American forefathers, Patrick Henry, had said "American liberty is the first interest I have at heart. American union is the second." Rejecting this premise, Lincoln was motivated, not by humanitarian reasons as is often asserted, but for the maintenance of power and to stave off the potential economic collapse that this separation would have potentially caused the North.

In his latest work, *The Great Yankee Coverup: What the North Doesn't Want You to Know About Lincoln's War!*, award-winning historian, author, and Sons of Confederate Veterans member Lochlainn Seabrook does an excellent job of outlining and describing many of the true causes that led to the secession movement and ultimately to war itself.

The War Between the States has fascinated me since I was in eleventh grade. This is one of many reasons that I joined the Sons of Confederate Veterans over twenty years ago. Upon joining the SCV I

The North doesn't want you to know that besides using black slaves to complete the dome on the U.S. Capitol at Washington, D.C., Liberal President Abraham Lincoln also forever altered the character of our government from that originally intended by the Founding Fathers.

have learned that much of what I was taught by the public school system was nothing more than the continuation of "reconstruction", a process that was begun 150 years ago by the North as a result of their victory in 1865. The purpose of the "reconstruction" era has been to justify their invasion of the South and, with their Northern propaganda agenda, to remake a singular "nation" that reflects their own image of how government and "the people" should relate to one another. By this process, the original design of our "union" has been effectively reversed, the principles embodied within the Declaration of Independence nullified, and the power of government transferred from "the people" of the various States to what Madison, discussing the fallacy of "implied powers", referred to as a "mixed-monarchy", wherein 545 men and women in Washington, DC have undertaken to tell the rest of us how we are to conduct our lives.

Lochlainn has done the South proud by superbly dispelling the myths surrounding this pivotal era in our country's history and by explaining how the Southern states not only possessed the constitutional right of secession, but desired to secede in a peaceful manner. Likewise, he soundly crushes many of the myths which students and most people of this country in general have been taught. I commend Lochlainn and his publisher Sea Raven Press for their efforts to put to rest the many misrepresentations of the Confederate South, and I highly recommend this book as well as the others they have published over the years. Works such as these allow the true mission of the Sons of Confederate Veterans to be accomplished, and they serve in educating the American people of the true facts and causes of the War of Northern Aggression.

As a lifelong resident of Limestone County, Alabama, I have over the years had to defend my stance on the reasons that my ancestors advocated secession and fought in the war. Most of these men that went and fought were not wealthy planters, but were instead farmers, merchants, students, and average people who were seeking only to defend their homes and their family's well being. When their communities were invaded by Yankee forces they had no choice but to stand up and fight in order to preserve their property and their God-given rights. These men were in many cases under-supplied, out-armed, and out-manned, but after four long years of fighting they left the field of battle with the knowledge that they had held their own and fought the good fight to defend the true "American tradition" of self-government.

Today these men are called "traitors" because of their attempt to start a new government. Were these not the same actions taken by men such as Washington, Jefferson, Henry, and Adams in 1776? Was it not these men who signed off on and established the uniquely American idea that

The North doesn't want you to know that their own slaves had few rights, that laws governing black Northern slaves were the strictest, cruelest, and most racist in the nation, and that Yankee slaves were routinely and brutally punished for even minor offences. This New York slave is being publicly burned at the stake for looking at a white woman.

"when government becomes destructive" of the ends for which it was created, it is their right to "alter", "abolish" or "throw" off that government and institute a new one that better suits them? They "seceded" from the King and Parliament of England in order to seek self-rule and to establish "that these united colonies are and of right ought to be free and independent States". "States" on par with the "State" of Great Britain. What changed in the years between 1788, when the constitution was ratified, and 1861 when it was effectively overthrown by the Lincoln administration? It's all explained here.

Lochlainn's work on the War has done history a great service.

Thomas V. Strain Jr.
Lt. Commander-in-Chief
Sons of Confederate Veterans
May 2015

14 ∾ THE GREAT YANKEE COVERUP

Former Yankee slave Frederick Douglass had nothing but disdain for Abraham Lincoln's insincere and exploitative relationship with African-Americans, even stating that the president's attitude toward blacks lacked "the genuine spark of humanity." During his public address to a largely Negro audience at the unveiling of the Freedmen's Monument in Lincoln Park, Washington, D.C., on April 14, 1876, for example, Douglass said of the Yankee chief executive: "It must be admitted, truth compels me to admit, even here in the presence of the monument we have erected to his memory, Abraham Lincoln was not, in the fullest sense of the word, either our man or our model. In his interests, in his associations, in his habits of thought, and in his prejudices, he was a white man. He was preeminently the white man's president, entirely devoted to the welfare of white men. He was ready and willing at any time during the first years of his administration to deny, postpone, and sacrifice the rights of humanity in the colored people to promote the welfare of the white people of this country." Thanks to The Great Yankee Coverup few Americans have ever heard of this speech, or of the widespread black disillusionment that followed Lincoln's election.

INTRODUCTION

It has long been self-evident to the more enlightened portion of the population that *all* of *mainstream* American history is biased, and therefore inaccurate and untrustworthy. This being true it should not shock anyone to learn that the America Civil War era is one of the most highly corrupt, distorted, edited, redacted, rewritten, bowdlerized, and expurgated periods in our history.

Who is responsible for this gross perversion of one of our country's most important and tragic periods, and why is this fact so little known? These questions were answered by my British cousin Winston Churchill, who once observed that "history is written by the victors."

The American Civil War is not what you were taught. This is not even its real or correct name.

In our case the culprits are, by and large, Yankee Liberals; members of the bi-coastal elite, headquartered in the left-leaning American Northeast and along the Pacific Coast. It is this progressive group—one that derogatorily views all of Middle America, including and especially the South, as insignificant "flyover zones"—that has not only completely controlled the Civil War narrative for the past 150 years, but which has also hijacked Southern history, rewriting it to fit their own socialist ideology and agenda.

The result has been what I call "The Great Yankee Coverup": the complete suppression of the facts about the Civil War in general, and the South and the Confederacy specifically. So thoroughly has this virulent anti-South movement buried the truth that many will at first view the contents of this book as fiction, or worse, purposeful fabrication. Even when they discover that I have gleaned most of this information from the writings and eyewitness accounts of both Southern *and* Northern 18th- and 19th-Century individuals, there are those on the Left who will still reject it, for cold hard facts are an anathema to the typical modern Liberal, who prefers his American history revised to match his sociopolitical views.

The open-minded and inquisitive, however, whether Liberal, Conservative, Libertarian, or Independent, will learn much from this book. They will discover, for example, that the South fought to preserve the Constitution while the North fought to overturn it; that the USA was created as a confederacy, that it was widely known as the "Confederate States of America," and that this is why the South adopted this name when it seceded from the Union; that the Southern states seceded legally with no intention of destroying the Union, and that their only goal was to perpetuate the original confederate republic formed by the Founding Fathers.

My readers will also learn that Confederate President Jefferson Davis was a Conservative who adopted a black child during the War and was already committed to abolishing slavery in early 1865, months before the War ended; that Union President Abraham Lincoln was a Liberal who barred blacks from the White House, consistently blocked black civil rights, wanted to put African-Americans in their own all-black state, spent his entire adult life trying to deport blacks, said that if there was a war between the races he would stand with his own, used slaves to complete the dome on the Capitol Building, referred to Native-Americans as "savages" and blacks as an "inferior race," and was a leader in, as well as a lifelong member of, the American Colonization Society, an organization whose stated goal was to make the U.S. "white from coast to coast."

The cover of Earl Browder's suppressed 1936 book *Lincoln and the Communists*. What pro-North writers will not tell you is that Republican President Abraham Lincoln was actually a socialistic white racist, supremacist, and separatist (who is still adored by progressives, racial bigots, communists, Marxists, and dictators); one who did more to damage, block, and delay black civil rights than anyone else in the 19th-Century. African-Americans, in fact, had no chance of *true* and *lasting* freedom as long as Lincoln was alive—which is why the Thirteenth Amendment came only after his death.

How does the North's self-reinforcing delusion, The Great Yankee Coverup, work?

One common and pernicious method is to simply flood the world with books, films, documentaries, TV shows, pamphlets, artwork, Websites, etc., that portray the Northern Union as "righteous" and the Southern Confederacy as "evil." Anti-South Yankees, Liberals, socialists, Marxists, communists, and even many uneducated Libertarians and Conservatives (both who should be friends of the South), churn out literally thousands of such items every year in an all-out effort to blanket the truth with lies and keep the facts from seeing the light of day.

The most serious offender in the literary field is, of course, the

These ten Ku Klux Klan members from around 1870—posing in front of a real skull and crossbones with hat bands that read "KKK"—were not from the South, as pro-North historians would have you believe. They were from the North—Watertown, New York, to be exact—and were known as "Watertown Division 289," just one of hundreds of KKK chapters that sprang up across the North after Lincoln's War. While anti-Southers want you to think they are one and the same, the truth is that the new modern Northern KKK has no connection with the old deceased Southern KKK: the former is an anti-black organization, the latter was an anti-Yankee organization which lasted only a little over three years, from late 1865 to early 1869, when Confederate General Nathan Bedford Forrest shut it down. The original Southern KKK was not even entirely Southern, for it borrowed many of its traditions, symbols, and rituals from Yankee organizations, one of them being the anti-Catholic, anti-immigrant group known as The Order of the Star Spangled Banner, founded in Boston, Massachusetts, in 1849. Revealingly, when the Banner folded in the early 1850s it evolved into the bigoted Know-Nothing Party, whose members supported, not Jefferson Davis and the South in the 1860 presidential election, but the racist "white man's party" of Abraham Lincoln and the North, the Republicans—the Liberal Party of the day.

much lauded university press, which is usually nothing more than a virulent left-wing (and, as such, anti-South) propaganda organization masquerading as a book publisher. In Hollywood we have the massive West Coast Liberal establishment, which spends an inordinate amount of its annual multibillion dollar budget on writing and filming movies that paint the Old and even the New South in the poorest light possible. And due to the democratic nature of the Web, anyone can write anything they wish about the South, the War, and the Confederacy as if it were true. There is no fact-checking, no research, no peer review for such material. Worse yet, it is all accepted by most of the public as authentic history, which is the goal of these malicious writers to begin with.

The truth is that nearly all of these pro-North products are based on nothing more than faulty, revisionist, heavily redacted information, for their authors merely copy and repeat the lies and fabrications of those who came before them, adding new falsities as they go. This is not just a problem in the U.S. The anti-South movement's literary works, movies, and blogs are international, poisoning the minds of people all over the world. Recently I heard a "highly educated" British journalist absurdly refer to Dixie as "the racist South" and "the home of the KKK"!⁵

Other popular methods of maintaining The Great Yankee Coverup include not only removing Confederate flags, statues, symbols, and monuments

Abraham Lincoln, a former Yankee newspaper editor, was well schooled in the art of manipulating the press, which is exactly what he did during his presidency. For example, he called the Southern Confederacy an "illegal organization," and the constitutional right of secession an "ingenious sophism," an "insidious debauching of the public mind," and a "sugar-coated invention" of the South—even though just a few years earlier he had publicly supported secession. Those who challenged his views he labeled "traitors" and "rebels." As Illinois Senator Stephen A. Douglas complained, Lincoln used this duplicitous language to great effect in his speeches as well, telling Northern audiences what they wanted to hear while telling Southern audiences what they wanted to hear, even though his words contradicted one another. Except for rare books like this one, you will never hear such facts, even though they are part of the public record. The Great Yankee Coverup has conveniently buried them under a mountain of Northern anti-South propaganda, hoping they will simply evaporate and be forgotten. Their plan has failed.

from public places, but also banning, shunning, ignoring, marginalizing, stigmatizing, criticizing, slandering, suppressing, and even criminalizing anything (e.g., books, films, etc.) or anyone who supports and promotes Southern and Confederate heritage. Since—like the news media, educational system, library system, and the majority of publishing houses—most historic Civil War sites in the South are now owned or run by Liberals, Yankees, or scallywags, the anti-South movement has a near complete lock on information that the public has access to. American children, for example, are taught only the North's version of the War, an insidious indoctrination that has been forced on our Southern schools since so-called "Reconstruction." Thus, the South-loathing gatekeepers not only conceal the truth, they are also free to shape it to fit their needs.

Some of their ploys are quite simple: label anything that is pro-South "controversial" and its supporters "racists," misguided members of the "Lost Cause" movement. This method carries over onto the Internet, where pro-South individuals, companies, and organizations are routinely banned from contributing to Civil War blogs, and are rudely ousted and barred from Civil War discussion groups. In such forums, where anti-South supporters hold sway, only one side of Lincoln's War is allowed to be expressed: the Northern one.

As for our 19th-Century Southern heros (such as Robert E. Lee), they are disrespectfully dismissed as "traitors," the Confederacy as an "illegal and treasonous government," and Old South Southerners as "illiterate, inbred, white trash." It does not

Among the biggest contributors to The Great Yankee Coverup today are the liberal university presses, which publish thousands of hackneyed, highly deceptive, poorly researched titles a year proclaiming Lincoln's greatness and the sanctity of the Union Cause. What the North does not want you to know, however, is that many of these same left-leaning schools were once bastions of racial bigotry. Dane Hall (above), for example, part of Harvard Law School at Cambridge, Massachusetts, was constructed from money made from the Yankee slave trade, as was nearby Faneuil Hall in Boston. Not surprisingly, like Lincoln, many of the early presidents of Northern colleges supported the racist American Colonization Society, among them Edward Everett (Harvard University), John Maclean Jr. (Princeton University), Jeremiah Day (Yale University), William A. Duer (Columbia College), and Henry Rutgers (for whom Rutgers University is named), among countless others who could be named.

matter that these charges are ridiculous and untrue. What matters to the politically correct is that these buzz words halt further discussion, as well as quickly kill off the Left's interest in factual Civil War books and honest Civil War writers. Yet these are the very people who are most in need of learning the truth about authentic Southern history.

Aztecs mercilessly sacrificing one of their slaves, a fellow Indian. The North would like you to believe that Southerners were the only Americans to ever practice slavery, and that "Southern slavery" was the world's most monstrous institution. This is just another one of the myths of The Great Yankee Coverup. Native-Americans were practicing slavery on one another for thousands of years prior to the arrival of Europeans, and in forms so sadistic and inhumane they defy description. American black slavery itself got its start in the North, where it was practiced far more savagely and far longer than in the South.

Though the truth has been expertly hidden from 21st-Century Americans, as this 1910 pamphlet by socialist dissident Burke McCarty shows, our 19th- and 20th-Century forebears were very well aware of who and what Lincoln was: a big government Liberal with socialistic tendencies, who surrounded himself with radical left-wingers. Many of his most passionate admirers, for instance, belonged to an extreme Marxist group known as the "Forty-Eighters." German socialist Karl Marx himself co-wrote an admiring book with fellow socialist Frederich Engels on Lincoln called *Abraham Lincoln und der Amerikanishe Bürgerkrieg* ("Abraham Lincoln and the American Civil War") Later Adolf Hitler, leader of the National Socialist German Workers' Party (that is, the Nazis), warmly acknowledged Lincoln's anti state's rights policies in his book *Mein Kampf*. That Lincoln was aligned with Hitler and other notable fascists and dictators is something no Liberal Northerner would ever want you to know. Conservative Southerners want you to know, however, and now you do.

What all of this means is that few if any mainstream bookstores or historic Civil War sites in the U.S. carry factual titles on Lincoln's War. Quite the contrary. You will find their shelves lined with defamatory anti-South works filled with errors, embellishments, misrepresentations, amplifications, distortions, deceptions, inaccuracies, exaggerations, contradictions, outright lies, and the usual battery of Yankee Civil War myths, all designed to denigrate the South, her people, her history, and her heritage. The result is that 99.99 percent of *authentic* Southern history books only come from small independent publishers or self-published authors.

By banning and suppressing genuine Civil War history books—like this one, written from the Southern perspective—the South-loathing supporters of The Great Yankee Coverup have been so successful that most reading this book are not aware that both the American slave trade and American slavery got their start in the North, and that the American abolition movement began in the South; that the Confederacy enlisted blacks before the Union, and that five times as many blacks fought for the South as for the North; that the Emancipation Proclamation freed no slaves and that this was not its true intention to begin with; that due to Lincoln's inhumane emancipation plan ("let 'em root, pig, or perish"), 25 percent of all Southern blacks died as a result of the Emancipation Proclamation; or that the Southern Confederacy was never officially shut down. The list goes on.

We have here proof not only that there is indeed a massive conspiracy to conceal the truth about the American Civil War, but that this conflict continues into the present.

One of the more popular jokes here in the South goes like this: "The Civil War isn't over. It's just halftime!" While this witticism is sure to evoke an approving laugh from just about any traditional Southerner, there is a reality behind it that is all too serious. However, the weapon now used is not a gun or a sword, but the written and spoken word. And while there is no officially declared war today, the lying, slander, and vitriol directed toward the South is just as vicious and absurd, if not more so, than it was in the 1860s. It is high time that this nonsense be exposed for what it is, and this is exactly what many proud and educated Southerners are now doing.

A Fulani woman and a Susu man in West Africa. Until recently both of these African peoples were aggressive slavers, capturing and enslaving untold thousands of fellow Africans annually. In some regions domestic African slave populations reached 90 percent. The North does not want you to know these facts, nor does it want you to learn that the institution continues across Africa to this day, with no sign of complete abolition in sight.

This book, along with the dozens of others I have penned on Lincoln's War, are my small contributions to that effort.

What are South-hating Liberals and uninformed Conservatives so afraid of? Why is it that they do not want you to know what really happened between November 6, 1860 (the day of Lincoln's election),

Blacks being turned away at a Union recruiting station. At first racist Lincoln refused to allow blacks—whom he referred to as an "inferior race"—to join the U.S. military. Later, with the drastic depletion of his white troops, he changed his mind, issuing what he tellingly called not a "black civil rights emancipation," but a "military emancipation," his infamous Emancipation Proclamation. Under Lincoln's ruthless black "enlistment" program, African-Americans were coerced to join the Union army at the tip of a gun barrel. Those who resisted (and many did) were bayoneted or shot where they stood. Those who acquiesced were subjected to Lincoln's ultra racist military polices, which included serving in segregated all-black units (often led by bigoted white officers), being paid half that of white Union soldiers, and being given medical attention only after whites had been treated. Little wonder that five times more blacks served in the Confederate army, which paid its black soldiers the same as its white soldiers, and fought its men in racially integrated troops.

and April 9, 1865 (the day of Lee's surrender)?

The Great Yankee Coverup, part of my personal counter propaganda campaign to restore the facts to our history books, will reveal the answer: the American Civil War was illegal, immoral, and unnecessary, and Abraham Lincoln was a dictatorial war criminal of the most despicable kind, directly responsible for the deaths of countless thousands of innocent people. In my opinion it is impossible that we will ever have a more dishonorable, fraudulent, and malevolent chief executive.

Please do not take my word for it. Read on and learn the truth for yourself. Not my truth, but the unvarnished truth of authentic history. Unlike the false, pretentious, flimsy "truth" disseminated by pro-North propagandists, this book preserves the objective reality of the War, a reality that cannot be tossed aside, hidden, buried, destroyed, forgotten, or pushed into oblivion—the ultimate goals of the enemies of the South.

True Southerners will never allow the flame of Southern truth to go out. We will keep it burning brightly until it finally illuminates and eventually quells every last one of the diabolical myths of *The Great Yankee Coverup*.

Lochlainn Seabrook
Nashville, Tennessee, USA
May 2015

Due to The Great Yankee Coverup you were never taught the most important facts about the Civil War. For example, despite the South's loss, the Confederacy was never officially shut down, and as such it still exists to this day. It is currently only dormant. Since their secession was legal under the Constitution, the Southern states technically only need hold elections and reopen the Confederate Congress to reactivate their government.

SECTION ONE

POLITICS & SECESSION

26 ∞ THE GREAT YANKEE COVERUP

The unscrupulous purveyors of The Great Yankee Coverup would rather you not know about white slavery in early America, that it got its start in the North, and that it was practiced by Yankees well into the Civil War period. If the truth got out, it would destroy the ridiculous myths they have invented about black slavery. The five year old child in this Victorian photo, for example, is a white Yankee slave girl by the name of Fannie Lawrence. According to official Northern records, she was baptized by Yankee preacher Henry Ward Beecher (a brother of the infamous novelist Harriet Beecher Stowe, author of the abolitionist fantasy *Uncle Tom's Cabin*) at Plymouth Church in Brooklyn, New York, in May 1863—in the midst of Lincoln's War. Fannie was henceforth known as a "redeemed slave child." Reverend Beecher was one of the few educated and rational Yankees of the 19th-Century, one rightly respected by many Southerners. Of the Northern myth of so-called "Southern slavery," he wrote: ". . . the importation of slaves was carried on by New England shipping merchants and defended by New England representatives; and when the proposition came before the Constitutional Convention [in 1787] for the prohibition of the slave-trade, New England voted for the clause that it should not be abolished until 1808. Thus the North shared with the South in the responsibility for the sin and shame of slavery, and it had no right, Pilate-like, to wash its hands and say, 'we are guiltless of this matter.' It was under sacred obligation to remain in the partnership and work for the renovation of the nation. As it was not right, so neither was it expedient."

FACT 1

THE NORTH DOESN'T WANT YOU TO KNOW THAT THE USA WAS ORIGINALLY & INTENTIONALLY FORMED AS A CONFEDERACY

The United States of America was officially born in 1781 with the ratification of our first Constitution, the Articles of Confederation. Why was it called the Articles of Confederation? Because the Founding Fathers had quite purposefully created our country as a Confederate Republic: a voluntary and friendly union of powerful, independent nation-states, operating under a weak, limited central government. Like so many others, Thomas Jefferson hoped that the U.S. would be a "lasting confederacy."

This is why Samuel Adams, for example, referred to the U.S. as a "Confederation" as early as 1776, in *The Federalist* (1787-1788) Alexander Hamilton called the U.S. the "American Confederacy," while James Madison called it "the present Confederation of the American States." In the same series of essays John Jay referred to the Southern states as the "Southern Confederacy" and Hamilton referred to the Northern states as the "Northern Confederacy." Like all other early American presidents and legislators, James Monroe too called the U.S. "the Confederacy" dozens if not hundreds of times throughout his writings and speeches.

In 1782 John Adams labeled the U.S. "the Confederacy," while Jefferson spoke of "our confederated fabric" in 1820, and was still referring to the U.S. as "our confederacy" in 1823, just three years before his death. In his 1837 Inaugural Address U.S. President Martin Van Buren referred to the country as "our confederacy."

Missouri Senator Thomas Hart Benton made mention of the U.S. "confederacy" in 1831 and again in 1844, in 1845 President James Knox Polk of Tennessee mentioned "our Confederacy" and "our confederation" in his First Inaugural Address, and in 1848 the future president of the Southern Confederacy, Jefferson Davis (named after Thomas Jefferson), spoke of the U.S. as "this glorious Confederacy," just twelve years prior to Lincoln's election. In 1849 Robert A. Toombs of Georgia referred to "this Confederacy" on the floor of the House.

And it was not just 19th-Century Southerners. Northerners too correctly called the U.S. "the Confederacy." In a December 24, 1847, letter, Governor Lewis Cass of Michigan used the phrase "the people of the Confederacy," and during his First Inaugural Address in 1853 American President Franklin Pierce of New Hampshire made reference to "this Confederacy." During his seventh and final debate with Lincoln on October 15, 1858, Illinois Senator Stephen A. Douglas referred to the U.S. as "a confederacy of sovereign and equal states."

Abraham Lincoln himself, a self-professed "northern man," labeled the nation "the Confederation" during this same debate with Douglas at Alton, Illinois, and as "the Confederacy," both during his New York address at the Cooper Institute on February 27, 1860, and as president-elect during his speech at Independence Hall, Philadelphia, Pennsylvania, on February 22, 1861.

In 1787 South Carolina Governor Thomas Pinckney called the USA "the confederated states," and in 1799 Samuel Phillips, president of the Massachusetts Senate, referred to his fellow states as "confederate states." In an 1832 speech South Carolina Governor James Hamilton Jr. spoke repeatedly of the USA as "our confederate states," and in 1833 Andrew Jackson made reference to "our confederation," calling it a union of "confederate states."

Even the U.S. Constitution of 1789 refers to our country, in its original form, as a Confederacy. Article 6 reads:

> All debts contracted and engagements entered into, before the adoption of this Constitution, shall be as valid against the United States under this Constitution, as under the Confederation.

It is clear that the Founding Generation continued to see the U.S. as a confederacy even after the adoption of the U.S. Constitution that year. One of these individuals was the country's first post-Articles chief executive, President George Washington, who referred to the newly refurbished government as "the new Confederacy." This clearly illustrates that he viewed the new (that is, today's) governmental system under the U.S. Constitution as being identical to the old one under the Articles of Confederation.

As proof that the U.S. Confederacy was a legitimate republic, we have only to look at the fact that it possessed all of the rights, powers, functions, and leaders of a confederacy, including a chief executive. In all, there were ten U.S. confederate presidents who held that office prior to George Washington—our first president under the later emerging U.S. Constitution.

The first president of the U.S. under the Articles of Confederation was Samuel Huntington of Connecticut, who served from September 28, 1779 to July 6, 1781. Though it was officially known as "President of the United States in Congress Assembled," the position was that of a true *confederate* chief executive.

What follows is a complete list of our first ten presidents and the dates they served. Note that under the Articles of Confederation there was no executive branch, making the office of "President of the Confederate Congress" far less onerous and rigorous than that of a modern U.S. president. As specified in Article 9 of the Articles of Confederation, each presidential term was limited to one year. Several men served partial terms, otherwise there would have only been eight presidents:

1. America's First Confederate President: Samuel Huntington of Connecticut (1731-1796): served from September 28, 1779, to July 6, 1781.
2. America's Second Confederate President: Thomas McKean of Delaware (1734-1817): served from July 10, 1781, to November 4, 1781.
3. America's Third Confederate President: John Hanson of Maryland (1715-1783): served from November 5, 1781, to November 4, 1782.
4. America's Fourth Confederate President: Elias Boudinot of New Jersey (1740-1821): served from November 4, 1782, to November 3, 1783.
5. America's Fifth Confederate President: Thomas Mifflin of Pennsylvania (1744-1800): served from November 3, 1783, to June 3, 1784.
6. America's Sixth Confederate President: Richard Henry Lee of Virginia (1732-1794): served from November 30, 1784, to

November 23, 1785.
7. America's Seventh Confederate President: John Hancock of Massachusetts (1737-1793): served from November 23, 1785, to June 6, 1786.
8. America's Eighth Confederate President: Nathaniel Gorham of Massachusetts (1738-1796): served from June 6, 1786, to November 13, 1786.
9. America's Ninth Confederate President: Arthur St. Clair of Pennsylvania (1737-1818): served from February 2, 1787, to October 29, 1787.
10. America's Tenth Confederate President: Cyrus Griffin of Virginia (1748-1810): served from January 22, 1788, to March 4, 1789.

Just two months later, on April 30, 1789, on the balcony of Federal Hall on Wall Street in New York City, Washington was sworn in as the first president of the United States of America under the newly effective U.S. Constitution, as mentioned, a republic he compared to the original government, calling both a "confederacy."[6]

Samuel Huntington of Connecticut was our first true president. The North does not want you to know this, however, because it would reveal the fact that the USA was intentionally formed by the Founders as a confederacy: a loose compact of all-powerful sovereign states operating under a weak limited central government.

FACT 2

THE NORTH DOESN'T WANT YOU TO KNOW THAT THE USA WAS ORIGINALLY KNOWN AS "THE CONFEDERATE STATES OF AMERICA"

The United States of America, which James Madison called "the present Confederation of the American States," was, from the very beginning, known to both American citizens and foreigners as not only "the confederate states," but more importantly as "the Confederate States of America."

In 1779, for example, in the midst of the American Revolutionary War, and two years before the original 13 colonies were first confederated under the Articles of Confederation in 1781, Reverend David S. Rowland, Minister of the Presbyterian Church at Providence, Rhode Island, published a small book with the unwieldy title: *Historical Remarks, with Moral Reflections: A Sermon Preached at Providence, June 6, 1779, Wherein are Represented, the Remarkable Dispensations of Divine Providence to the People of these States, Particularly in the Rise and Progress of the Present War, Between the Confederate States of America, and Great-Britain.*

Three years later, in 1782, an anonymous English author using the pseudonym "a Man of No Party," referred to the USA as "the confederate states of America." That same year minister Robert Smith of Pequea, Pennsylvania, penned a book entitled: *The Obligations of the Confederate States of North America to Praise God.* This was 79 years before the official formation of the Southern Confederacy in 1861.

A half century later, writing in the early 1830s, French aristocrat and tourist Alexis de Tocqueville made the following statements after visiting the U.S., all some 30 years prior to the formation of the Southern Confederacy:

> . . . the confederate states of America [that is, the United States of America] had been long accustomed to form a portion of one empire before they had won their independence: they had not contracted the habit of governing themselves, and their national

prejudices had not taken deep root in their minds. Superior to the rest of the world in political knowledge, and sharing that knowledge equally among themselves, they were little agitated by the passions which generally oppose the extension of federal authority in a nation, and those passions were checked by the wisdom of the chief citizens.

The plain fact is that *all* of America's early presidents, statesmen, politicians, judicial scholars, and citizens viewed the United States as a confederate republic. This even included 18th- and 19th-Century Liberals, all who unfailingly maintained that the country was a "confederation of sovereign states." This is indeed why nearly everyone endearingly referred to the USA variously as "the Confederate States," "our Confederacy," "our Confederation," the "American Confederacy," or most accurately, "the Confederate States of America."[7]

Highly educated French aristocrat, libertarian, statesman, and historian, Alexis de Tocqueville, like many other early Victorians both foreign and domestic, correctly referred to antebellum America as "the Confederate States of America."

FACT 3

THE NORTH DOESN'T WANT YOU TO KNOW THAT THE U.S. WAS MEANT TO BE A BODY OF "STATES UNITED" NOT "UNITED STATES"

During the 1789 ratification process of the new U.S. Constitution, the various colonies made it clear that the document was not "a Constitution for the United States" under democracy. It was "a Constitution for States United" under confederation. As Jefferson Davis later remarked concerning the Philadelphia Convention in 1787:

> It was as 'United States'—not as a state, or united people—that these colonies—still distinct and politically independent of each other—asserted and achieved their independence of the mother-country. As 'United States' they adopted the Articles of Confederation, in which the separate sovereignty, freedom, and independence of each was distinctly asserted. They were 'united States' when Great Britain acknowledged the absolute freedom and independence of each, distinctly and separately recognized by name. France and Spain were parties to the same treaty, and the French and Spanish idioms still express and perpetuate, more exactly than the English, the true idea intended to be embodied in the title—*les États Unis, or los Estados Unidos*—the States united.

In other words, the Founding Fathers did not view the U.S. Confederacy as "the whole mass of the people of the states" (that is, as a democracy ruled by the majority), but rather as the American states united by the original compact under confederation (that is, as a republic ruled by law), a vitally important distinction.

In 1868, three years after the end of Lincoln's War, former Confederate Vice President Alexander H. Stephens wrote similarly:

> [Our government] . . . is a Government instituted by States and for States, and . . . all the functions it possesses, even in its direct action on the individual citizens of the several States, spring from and depend upon a Compact between the States constituting it. It

is, therefore, a Government of States and for States. The final action upon the very first resolution . . . shows that the object of the [Philadelphia] Convention [of 1787] was to form a Government of States. 'The Government of the United States' ought to consist, they declared, 'of a Supreme Legislature, Judiciary and Executive.' This is the same as if they had declared 'the Government of the States United, ought to consist,' etc. The first Constitution, we have seen, was a Government of States. The States in Congress assembled passed all laws, made all treaties, and exercised all powers vested in them jointly. No measure could be passed without the equal voice of each State, however small. Delaware had the same influence as New York, Massachusetts, or Virginia, and in this respect I maintain there is no essential change in the new Constitution.[8]

Conservative Confederate Vice President Alexander H. Stephens understood and confirmed that the U.S. Constitution was not intended to created a government of the United States, as a whole, but rather a government of the States United, that is, as individual sovereigns. Liberal Lincoln went against the Founders by trying to overturn this idea, much to the detriment of Americans both North and South.

FACT 4

THE NORTH DOESN'T WANT YOU TO KNOW THAT NEW ENGLAND, NOT THE SOUTH, WAS THE FIRST REGION TO TRY BOTH CONFEDERATION & SECESSION

One of the greatest Yankee myths is that the Southern states were the first to "rebel" by attempting to secede from the Union and institute a confederacy. The truth is that long before the formation of the Southern Confederacy in 1861, the New England states had been seriously discussing these two ideas, and were in fact the first to attempt both. During the early 1800s alone, New England would try at least three times to secede from the Union, while Massachusetts attempted secession on four different occasions, all—it should be noted—without any resistance from the Southern states, or any other state for that matter.

New England was already displaying great enthusiasm for the idea of confederation over a century before the formation of the United States of America. In 1856 historian James V. Marshall wrote of New England's first experiment with the idea, a 43 year long confederation formed in the year 1643—as was noted by, among others, Thomas Jefferson:

> In 1643, the colonies of New Haven, Plymouth, Massachusetts, and Connecticut, entered into a confederacy, under the name of the United Colonies of New England, which continued till 1686. It was then stipulated that two commissioners from each colony should meet annually, to decide on matters of common concern; that the votes of six members should bind the whole; that in every war, each colony should furnish its quota of men money and provisions, in proportion to the number of people; and that every colony should be distinct, and have exclusive jurisdiction within its own territory. Though the strong members of this confederacy did not always act in a liberal manner toward their associates, yet it increased the power and security of the whole.[9]

FACT 5

THE NORTH DOESN'T WANT YOU TO KNOW THAT THE NEW ENGLAND CONFEDERACY WAS THE PROTOTYPE FOR BOTH THE US CONFEDERACY & THE SOUTHERN CONFEDERACY

On May 29, 1843, John Quincy Adams gave a speech before the Massachusetts Historical Society called "The New England Confederacy of 1643." The occasion was the "celebration of the second centennial anniversary of that event." Said Adams:

> The New England confederation originated in the Plymouth colony, and was probably suggested to them by the example which they had witnessed, and under which they had lived for several years in the United Netherlands. . . . At the formation of the New England union . . . [it] then consisted of four separate independent communities [Massachusetts, Plymouth, Connecticut, and New Haven], in a great measure self-formed; the vital principle common to them all being religious contention—and the quickening spirit, equal rights, freedom of thought and action, and personal independence. . . . [After entering] into a firm and perpetual league of friendship and amity for offence and defence, mutual advice and succor upon all just occasions . . . [they were henceforth] called by the name of the United Colonies of New England. . . . The New England confederacy of 1643 was the model and prototype of the North American [U.S.] confederacy of 1774. . . . Of the North American [U.S.] confederacy, self-constituted in the progress of the [American] revolution which converted the thirteen English colonies into independent states, New England forms a constituent part . . .

In short, according to one of our own presidents, the New England Confederacy laid the groundwork for the creation of the U.S. Confederacy in 1781. And this was, of course, the model for the Southern Confederacy in 1861—more proof that the South did not secede to destroy the government of the Founders, but to preserve it.

The brewing issue finally culminated in the Hartford Convention, a secession conference held from December 15, 1814, to January 5, 1815. Here, 26 Federalist delegates (Liberals) met secretly to not only propose amendments that would lessen the influence of the South, but to discuss leaving the Union in order to form a new and separate confederacy, the "New England Confederacy," as they called it, one they hoped would eventually include New York, Pennsylvania, and even Nova Scotia.

Among the convention's recommendations were allowing the states in the New England Confederacy greater military control, as well as amendments to the U.S. Constitution that would limit the powers of Congress and the executive.

The New England Confederacy was in "rebellion" from its very inception: it opposed the War of 1812 and refused to obey President James Madison's call for troops. All of this took place nearly a half century before the secession of the Southern states and the formation of the Southern Confederacy in 1861. One furious anti-South Massachusetts official, Senator Timothy Pickering—who once referred to Southern hero Thomas Jefferson as a "revolutionary monster," and accused him of cruelty, cowardice, turpitude, corruption, and baseness—spoke for all of the members of the Hartford Convention when he called for a racist secession:

> I will rather anticipate a new Confederacy, exempt from the corrupt and corrupting influence of the aristocratic Democrats [Conservatives] of the South. There will be—and our children at farthest will see it—a separation. The white and black population will mark the boundary. The British Provinces, even with the assent of Britain, will become members of the Northern confederacy. A continued tyranny of the present ruling sect will precipitate that event.

New England eventually decided against secession, though only for economic reasons.

The important point, however, is that had she desired to do so, New England could have seceded legally and peacefully—and unlike Lincoln's violent, militaristic reaction to Southern secession, the South would not have stood in New England's way. For there was never any doubt among Americans at the time that the individual states were independent nations, and that secession was therefore a constitutional right.[10]

Politician Timothy Pickering of Massachusetts was one of the primary leaders in the Yankee secession movement, which arose in the early 1800s, decades before the South seceded. The new country was to be called the "New England Confederacy," and include New York, Pennsylvania, and Nova Scotia. No one bullied the New England states, let alone threatened them with violence and war, for considering leaving the Union. It was simply accepted that under the Constitution they were free to separate and even return later if they so desired.

FACT 6

THE NORTH DOESN'T WANT YOU TO KNOW THAT SECESSION WAS LEGAL IN 1860

In the mid 1800s secession was perfectly legal, which makes Lincoln's War on the South illegal and everything that the North inflicted on the Southern people between 1861 and 1877 (the year "Reconstruction" ended) a war crime.

To begin with, secession is one of the rights of states, and states' rights are assured and openly declared in the Declaration of Independence, issued by the U.S. Congress on July 4, 1776, and penned by Southern icon and Founding Father Thomas Jefferson. The Declaration's focus on states' rights and the concomitant right of secession was carried forward by the U.S. Confederacy (1781-1789) into the Articles of Confederation, which were ratified March 1, 1781. In Article Two, the concept of states' rights is plainly laid out:

> Each state retains its sovereignty, freedom, and independence, and every power, jurisdiction, and right, which is not by this Confederation expressly delegated to the United States, in Congress assembled.

The Founders did not neglect the issue of states' rights when they replaced the Articles with the Constitution of the United States of America on March 4, 1789. In fact they considered it important enough to include it as a separate amendment in the Bill of Rights (the first ten Amendments), which went into effect in 1791. Indeed, the Tenth Amendment is, in its entirety, devoted solely to states' rights:

> The powers not delegated to the United States by the Constitution, nor prohibited by it to the States, are reserved to the States respectively, or to the people.

In other words, the national government was only allowed to exercise those powers bestowed on it by the people. What are these powers? They are explicitly defined in Article Four, Section Four:

> The United States shall guarantee to every state in this Union a republican form of government, and shall protect each of them against invasion; and on application of the Legislature, or of the executive (when the Legislature cannot be convened), against domestic violence.

As laid out here, in essence the only power originally granted to the national government by the people was the power to protect them against the formation of state dictatorships, foreign invasion, and internal disturbances (for example, riots). Outside of these three obligations (basically, the defense of lives, rights, and property), all sovereign power was to remain in the hands of the people.

In short, if the individual states of the U.S. were intended to be sovereign nation-states, as our government documents clearly reveal they were, and are, then the rights of both accession (joining the Union) and secession (leaving the Union) are legal.[11]

Some have countered that because the right of secession was not clearly spelled out in the U.S. Constitution, it is therefore illegal. Yet there is nothing in that document stating that it is not legal.

The real question is, why did the Founding Fathers leave out any direct reference to secession? The answer is that it was so well-known and accepted at the time that they did not feel it was necessary. Confederate President Jefferson Davis answered the question this way:

> It was not necessary in the Constitution to affirm the right of secession, because it was an attribute of sovereignty, and the states had reserved all which they had not delegated [to the central government].

Actually, up until 1865, secession was the most frequently discussed political issue in both the United States and the Confederate States. Thus to the Framers and the general populace, it was merely another common law that was universally recognized and accepted by every American citizen. As Yankee constitutional scholar William Rawle said in 1829: "though not expressed, [it] was mutually understood."[12]

FACT 7

THE NORTH DOESN'T WANT YOU TO KNOW THAT ABRAHAM LINCOLN ONCE HELD SECESSION TO BE LEGAL, "SACRED," & "VALUABLE"

Secession is lawful, Lincoln once asserted! He even called it a "most sacred right." On January 12, 1848, in a speech before the U.S. House of Representatives, he declared:

> Any people anywhere, being inclined and having the power, have the right to rise up, and shake off the existing government, and form a new one that suits them better. This is a most valuable, a most sacred right—a right which, we hope and believe, is to liberate the world. Nor is this right confined to cases in which the whole people of an existing government may choose to exercise it. Any portion of such people that can may revolutionize, and make their own of so much of the territory as they inhabit.

When it was politically expedient to change his mind, Lincoln, of course, did just that. As U.S. president 13 years later, on July 4, 1861, in his "Message to Congress in Special Session," he called the new Southern Confederacy an "illegal organization," and the constitutional right of secession an "ingenious sophism," an "insidious debauching of the public mind," and a "sugar-coated invention" of the South. Those who challenged these views were labeled "traitors" and "rebels."

This is how Confederate soldiers got the epithet "Johnny Rebel," and how the name of Lincoln's War, "the War of Rebellion," came about. It is also why, after the War, Confederate officers were charged with "treason": for believing in, and acting on, the legal right of secession. Even the term Copperhead (meaning a Northerner who sympathized with the South) was anti-South: ridiculously and incorrectly, it likened such supporters to the deadly venomous snake of the same name.[13]

FACT 8

THE NORTH DOESN'T WANT YOU TO KNOW THAT THE USA IS A VOLUNTARY UNION OF STATES

Since the USA began as, and still is, a confederacy, and because a confederacy is a *voluntary* union, new territories cannot be forced to accede (enter the Union). They must accede voluntarily. It then naturally follows that they cannot be forced to remain in the Union, but have a right to secede (leave the Union) voluntarily if and when they so desire.

This is a form of reasoning that a third-grader could understand. Yet it was (and still is) beyond some of the greatest minds in the North!

The South fought, in great part, to maintain the voluntary nature of the Union. The North fought to destroy it.

Indeed, many foreigners have shown a far greater understanding of the voluntary nature of the American Union—and her concomitant confederate rights of accession and secession—than our own politicians. One of these was French aristocrat Alexis de Tocqueville, who wrote the following in the early 1800s:

> The [American] Union was formed by the voluntary agreement of States; and, in uniting together, they have not forfeited their nationality, nor have they been reduced to the condition of one and the same people. If one of the States chose to withdraw its name from the contract, it would be difficult to disprove its right of doing so; and the Federal Government would have no means of maintaining its claims directly either by force or by right.[14]

FACT 9

THE NORTH DOESN'T WANT YOU TO KNOW THAT IT WAS LINCOLN'S ELECTION ON NOVEMBER 6, 1860, WHICH TRIGGERED THE SECESSION OF THE SOUTHERN STATES

In one of the more bizarre incidents in American history, after ascending to the White House, Abraham Lincoln chose to dismiss the aforementioned bold facts, as if none of them were true or indeed had ever even existed. Like big government Liberals today, he detested the Founding Fathers' individualistic concept of confederation, with its accompanying entitlements of states' rights and secession.

It is little wonder then that the Southern Confederacy got its start on November 6, 1860, the day white supremacist Lincoln, a Republican (the Liberal Party at the time), was elected America's sixteenth president on a platform promising *not* to interfere with slavery—as he clearly states in his Inaugural Address on March 4, 1861, and as was asserted obliquely in the 1860 Republican Party Platform.[15]

It was Lincoln's election in the Autumn of 1860 that decided the question of Southern secession and which launched the Confederacy, not slavery. Southerners simply could not abide the thought of living under the rule of a liberal, Constitution-loathing, anti-South autocrat.

FACT 10

The North Doesn't Want You to Know that the South Named Its New Republic After one of the Early Names for the United States: "The Confederate States of America"

The Southern Confederacy possessed 13 seceded states in all, which were symbolized by a 13-star circle on its First National Flag. This, of course, was the same number of colonial states that had seceded from England to form the first Confederate States of America in 1781, and which were astrally symbolized on the U.S. Confederate flag of that period, and which is still known as the "Betsy Ross Flag."

The first official flag of the U.S., the "Betsy Ross" had a 13-star circle representing the colonies of Delaware, Pennsylvania, New Jersey, Georgia, Connecticut, Massachusetts, Maryland, South Carolina, New Hampshire, Virginia, New York, North Carolina, and Rhode Island.

Furthermore, despite a few significant alterations, the Southern Confederacy very precisely patterned its Constitution on the Constitution of the United States, a document that was, in turn, built around our country's first Constitution, the Articles of Confederation, formulated during the period of American Confederation (1781-1789).

Lastly, like the USA, the CSA was intentionally formed to be what Thomas Jefferson had decades earlier called a "lasting confederacy": a perpetual union of powerful autonomous states existing under a small limited central government.

It is obvious then why the Southern Confederate Founding Fathers gave their new republic the name "the Confederate States of America." As we have seen, this was the name given to the original USA by both American citizens and foreigners, and more loosely by the American Founding Fathers and countless subsequent statesmen and politicians, from George Washington and Thomas Jefferson to Jefferson Davis and Abraham Lincoln.

Thus, *the second Confederate States of America (1861) was meant to be a continuation of the first or original Confederate States of America (1781)*, not a rebellion intent on "destroying the United States," as anti-South critics continue to misleadingly assert.[16]

The 13-star "Betsy Ross" flag, the first official flag of the USA.

The 13-star "First National" flag, the first official flag of the CSA, patterned on the USA's "Betsy Ross" flag. Both republics were created as confederacies and both were known as "the Confederate States of America," ironclad historical facts the North does not want you to know.

FACT 11

THE NORTH DOESN'T WANT YOU TO KNOW THAT THE CONFEDERATE STATES OF AMERICA OF 1861 HAD THE SUPPORT OF EUROPE

Mainstream history books would have us believe that the Southern Confederacy could not secure the support of Europe because she "practiced slavery." But this is false. The real reason Europe hesitated to give the South diplomatic recognition was because it feared offending and possibly provoking the U.S. into war, a frightening scenario that at one point almost became a reality.

Through Lincoln's secretary of state, William H. Seward, Lincoln privately threatened war on any nation that interfered with his illegal invasion of the South, in particular England and France, where sympathy for the Confederacy was strongest. Lincoln's apprehension was warranted: England's and France's ruling classes were always highly interested in and supportive of the Confederate Cause, while the English population as a whole expressed "widespread sentiment" in favor of recognizing the Confederacy as a sovereign nation.

Via Lincoln's orders, William H. Seward privately warned a Confederate-sympathetic Europe to avoid giving aid or recognition to the South under threat of war.

It was Lincoln's menacing warning, in place throughout the duration of the conflict, that prevented "neutral" Europe from publicly supporting "belligerent" Dixie, and which in turn prolonged the War, caused thousands of unnecessary deaths, and aided in the South's eventual downfall.[17]

FACT 12

THE NORTH DOESN'T WANT YOU TO KNOW THAT THE CONFEDERATE BATTLE FLAG IS NOT A SYMBOL OF SLAVERY OR WHITE SUPREMACY

From the very beginning Dixie has been a multiracial, multiethnic, multicultural society, as is obvious from the region's military rolls, created during Lincoln's War. Under the beautiful Confederate Battle Flag (designed by my cousin Confederate General Pierre G. T. Beauregard), every known race donned Rebel gray or butternut and proudly and bravely defended Dixie against the Yankee invaders.

This proves to the world like nothing else can, that from the beginning the Confederacy fought, not to exploit and oppress the black race or any other race, but for the constitutional rights and personal freedom of all her people. Those who say anything different are either lying or are ignorant of genuine Southern history, plain and simple.

Some from the anti-Confederate Flag movement, like the race-baiting, racially intolerant Northern-based NAACP, know full well the true meaning of what we in Dixie call the "Southern Cross." Unfortunately, such groups (which even other blacks, like Reverend Jesse Lee Peterson, have labeled "hate groups") have a vested financial interest in fanning the flames of racism, for without the racial divisiveness created by their fake "race war," the world's race-merchants would go bankrupt.

Our most racist liberal president, Abraham Lincoln, thought along similar lines. He, along with the Radicals (that is, abolitionists) in his party, believed that by pitting whites and blacks against each other, the resulting tension, emotion, and fear would divide and weaken the South, allowing him to manipulate and overcome her people easier. Happily, Lincoln's attempt to poison Southern race relations failed, for the majority of whites and blacks saw through the ruse and remained loyal to one another both during and after his War.

The Confederate Battle Flag turns out to be anything but a symbol of slavery or white supremacy. Those who created it never intended it to have these meanings, and those who fought under it never thought of it in this way either. The descendants of those soldiers today have also never perceived it in this manner, as I myself can testify.

If anything it would be more accurate to call our flag a symbol of racial inclusiveness and multiculturalism, one founded on the Christian principles extolled by Jesus, whose main tenants were love and universal brotherhood. The Confederate Battle Flag itself was designed around the Christian crosses of Great Britain's flag (Saint George's Cross), Scotland's flag (Saint Andrew's Cross), and Ireland's flag (Saint Patrick's Cross).

Our beloved Battle Flag then, the winsome Southern Cross, is an emblem of not only small government, capitalism, personal liberty, and self-government, but also of American patriotism, strict constitutionalism, Christian love, and Southern heritage. Indeed, these are the very reasons that Conservative Confederate President Jefferson Davis described the Southern Confederacy as "the last best hope of liberty."

As such, the Confederate Battle Flag is one that all Southerners, and all lovers of freedom, can revere unreservedly, as well as display with pride and honor whenever and wherever possible. Conservative Founder and Southern abolitionist Thomas Jefferson, the "Father of the Declaration of Independence," would heartily approve.[18]

SECTION TWO

LINCOLN'S WAR

50 ∾ THE GREAT YANKEE COVERUP

New Englanders such as Ralph Waldo Emerson, Henry David Thoreau, and Louisa May Alcott likened Yankee abolitionist John Brown to a saint, and even to Jesus! But the truth is that the madman from Connecticut was closer to Satan than anything else. His plan to free all of the South's slaves, enlist them in his army, then march them across Dixie and kill as many white people as possible, was pronounced insane even by other Northerners, like Lincoln and Frederick Douglass. After pointlessly murdering and wounding dozens of people from Kansas to Virginia, Brown was finally captured by future Confederate officer, U.S. Colonel Robert E. Lee, at Harper's Ferry, in October 1859. The Yankee's violent bloody raid on the Southern town was a tragic failure in which one of his own sons was killed—along with a black man that had refused to join his band of lunatics. Brown was convicted of treason, and swung on the hangman's noose, a just end for an unjust man. Of course The Great Yankee Coverup wants you to believe that Brown was a genius. But trying to abolish slavery in Virginia, the birthplace of the American abolition movement, a state whose citizens had been trying to stamp out the institution since the early 1600s, is what we Southerners call stupidity.

FACT 13

THE NORTH DOESN'T WANT YOU TO KNOW THAT THE NORTH, NOT THE SOUTH, STARTED THE SO-CALLED "CIVIL WAR"

It is true that the South fired the first volley on April 12, 1861, during the War's opening conflict at Fort Sumter, South Carolina. But this does not also mean that she launched the conflict. In fact, there is indisputable evidence showing the opposite; that the South was tricked into firing the initial salvo, and that it was the North who instigated hostilities, marking the beginning of the War.

The idea for hoaxing the Confederacy originated with Lincoln's secretary of the navy, Gideon Welles, who slyly advised the president that "it is very important that the Rebels strike the first blow in the conflict." Lincoln's assistant secretary of the navy, Gustavus Fox, then took Welles' idea and worked out the details of the plan. Writing to Montgomery Blair (soon to be Lincoln's postmaster general) on February 23, 1861, Fox said:

> I simply propose three tugs, convoyed by light-draft men-of-war.
> . . . The first tug to lead in empty, to open their fire.

Fox's plan never materialized, however, because the Rebels, having been grossly misled and lied to about Lincoln's intentions, went ahead and bombed and captured the fort first. What led up to this?

From the start Lincoln had promulgated a fiction that his Union soldiers stationed at Fort Sumter were "starving" and needed to be "reprovisioned." This was a bald lie, however, for Confederate General Pierre G. T. Beauregard had allowed Lincoln's troops to purchase groceries in Charleston up until April 5. Additionally, every day "the people of Charleston sent to Sumter a boat load of food supplies, fresh meats, fowls, fruits, vegetables, etc." The Union soldiers on the island were thus well-stocked with victuals and were in no way "starving," as some Northern newspapers had been telling their eager readers.

Should the "starving" fort be "reprovisioned"? Lincoln claimed so, but his cabinet, including the attorney general and his secretaries of the interior, war, navy, and state, all advised against it.

Abolitionists, Northern members of the opposing party, and Union military brass from across the U.S. were nearly all of the same mind. Horace Greeley's newspaper, the New York *Tribune*, called on Lincoln to avoid the use of force and allow the Southern states to secede in peace, while Illinois Democrat Stephen A. Douglas said that the Union troops "should be instantly withdrawn."

On March 28 the greatly respected Yankee General Winfield Scott had advised his president to not only evacuate Fort Sumter, but the nearby Union-held garrison Fort Pickens, as well. "Abandon these forts. They're militarily useless to us, and such action would politically benefit the U.S.," Scott wisely urged Lincoln. According to Simon Cameron, Lincoln's secretary of war: "All the officers within Fort Sumter . . . [also] express this opinion . . .," including the commanding officer, Yankee Major Robert Anderson, who was still awaiting orders there. Caleb B. Smith, Lincoln's secretary of the interior, agreed. "If you send in provisions it will trigger a civil war."

What his cabinet did not seem to realize was that this is exactly what Lincoln wanted. And the "starving fort" tale was the very trigger mechanism Lincoln needed to initiate it!

On April 12, against the advice of his own cabinet and the sentiment of most of the Northern people, Lincoln sent a provisions supply ship to Fort Sumter. Accompanying it were several armed warships bristling with heavily armed troops. Lincoln had meticulously planned out every detail and knew what was about to happen.

Seeing the Federal fleet moving through Charleston harbor toward Fort Sumter, Confederate troops let loose their cannon. For a full 36 hours they bombarded the island, expecting at any moment to receive enemy fire. But the expected Yankee response never came. Why? Because Lincoln had ordered his men not to. It was all a hoax, one meant to goad the Confederacy into firing the first shot.

The end result was exactly what Lincoln had intended: the South appeared to the world to be the instigator. Now the onus of initiating war lay with the Confederacy.

On May 1, 1861, three weeks after his heinous deed at Sumter had been committed, Lincoln acknowledged the devilish connivance in a letter to Fox. While Fox was disappointed that his and Welles' plan had not come off exactly as planned, Lincoln was elated:

> I sincerely regret that the failure of the attempt to provision Fort Sumter should be the source of annoyance to you . . .
> You and I both anticipated that the cause of the country would be advanced by making the attempt to provision Fort Sumter even if it should fail; and it is no small consolation now to feel that our anticipation is justified in the results.

What "results?" The inauguration of a war he so desperately wanted! Even Lincoln's own authorized biographers, John G. Nicolay and John Hay, admitted that:

> When the President determined on war, and with the purpose of making it appear that the South was the aggressor, he took measures . . .

Lincoln's so-called "measures" were nothing more than pure evil trickery.

As the public too soon learned, the entire Fort Sumter event turned out to be a cleverly calculated conspiracy—as one Northern newspaper described it—to incite the South into shooting first. In this way the Confederacy was seen as the aggressor, a hot-headed rebel who had fired on Old Glory and tried to prevent food from reaching "starving" U.S. soldiers.

Here then was the perfect justification for invading the South. For with the "Rebel attack on the U.S. flag," as Lincoln told Congress,

> no choice was left but to call out the war power of the Government, and so to resist force employed for its destruction by force for its preservation.

In 1867, six years later, Southern fire-eater Edward A. Pollard wrote of this flashpoint in American history:

> The point of the [Lincoln] government was to devise some artifice for the relief of Fort Sumter, short of open military reinforcements, decided to be impracticable, and which would have the effect of inaugurating the war by a safe indirection and under a plausible and

convenient pretence. The device was at last conceived.

Four years later, in his Second Inaugural Address, on March 4, 1865, Lincoln was still trying to maintain his "convenient pretence" before the public. Here he had the gall to claim that both the South and the North had tried to avoid bloodshed,

> but one of them would make war rather than let the nation survive, and the other would accept war rather than let it perish; and the war came.

And Northerners wonder why we call him "Dishonest Abe"?

The idea that the war simply "came," and that this was due to the aggressive actions of those he preposterously called "insurgents," is absurd and an insult to all intelligent people. Yet it was in this exact way that the South has been held criminally responsible for a war it did not begin—or want. Let us bear in mind, as President Jefferson Davis said:

> He who makes the assault is not necessarily he that strikes the first blow or fires the first gun.

How true. In the end, as Pollard notes:

> The battle of Sumter had been brought on by the Washington Government by a trick too dishonest and shallow to account for the immense display of sentiment in the North that ensued. The event afforded indeed to many politicians in the North a most flimsy and false excuse for loosing passions of hate against the South that had all along been festering in the concealment of their hearts.

Yes, the South fired the first shot. But the North intentionally and guilefully tricked her into it, launching a full-scale war based solely on deception and a tiny skirmish in which not a single person was even injured. Thus, as Confederate army chaplain Robert Lewis Dabney so aptly observed, the "Civil War was conceived in duplicity, and brought forth in iniquity."[19]

FACT 14

The North Doesn't Want You to Know that the Civil War Was Not a Civil War

Webster defines a civil war as a "conflict between opposing groups of citizens of the same country." This was clearly not the case with America's War of 1861, which here in the South we more correctly refer to as the War Against Northern Aggression, or the Second Revolutionary War.

By February 1861, two months before the start of the conflict, seven Southern states had seceded from the Union, forming the Confederate States of America, or CSA (four more, as well as portions of two other Southern states, would also eventually secede). Patterned on the original U.S., which was also known as "the Confederate States of America," this, the second CSA, was a legitimate, constitutionally formed, sovereign confederate republic, and was therefore no longer connected with the USA. This makes the term "Civil War" entirely erroneous when used for the War of 1861. For it was not a civil war, but a regular war; one fought between opposing groups of citizens of two separate and independent countries, two confederacies, in fact.

Why does the North push the phrase "Civil War" then? Because it is vital to propping up one of the most important pillars of The Great Yankee Coverup; namely, that by seceding, the Southern states were guilty of an unconstitutional act of treason, one that threatened to "destroy the Union." Thus, according to Liberal Lincoln and his modern leftist followers, a full scale military invasion of Dixie was needed in order to bring the Southern states back into the fold and "preserve the Union." Supposedly adding to this need to wage war was the fact that two years in, Lincoln altered the character of the War from a political one to a moral one, the new purpose being to abolish Southern slavery.

As we have seen, however, secession was—and still is—legal. Once one becomes aware of this fact, the entire myth of the "Civil War" falls like the house of cards that it is.[20]

FACT 15

THE NORTH DOESN'T WANT YOU TO KNOW THAT THE CIVIL WAR WASN'T OVER SLAVERY

According to pro-North writers, the North fought the South to "preserve the Union" and "destroy slavery," while the South fought the North to "destroy the Union" and "preserve slavery." That this 150 year old view is nothing but anti-South propaganda, designed to perpetuate The Great Yankee Coverup, is easily provable.

It is patently clear to all rational thinking individuals that slavery had nothing to do with the Civil War. For one thing, if slavery had been the cause, the War would have ended on September 22, 1862, when Lincoln issued his Preliminary Emancipation Proclamation, or at least by January 1, 1863, when he issued his Final Emancipation Proclamation. Yet, the bloody, illegal, and unnecessary conflict continued for another two years. If the War was about abolition and America's slaves were now free, why go on fighting?

Furthermore, it would have cost ten times less to simply free America's slaves than to go to war. Not even the megalomaniacal Lincoln, with all of his psychological problems and emotional disabilities, was mentally unbalanced enough to overlook this important fact.

However, the most damning evidence against the Yankee myth that "slavery triggered the Civil War" comes from the top political and military leaders of both the Confederacy and the Union. Here is how C.S. President Jefferson Davis put it:

> The truth remains intact and incontrovertible, that the existence of African servitude was in no wise the cause of the conflict, but only an incident. In the later controversies that arose, however, its effect in operating as a lever upon the passions, prejudices, or sympathies of mankind, was so potent that it has been spread like a thick cloud over the whole horizon of historic truth.

To the last day of his life the Confederacy's celebrated vice president, Alexander H. Stephens, declared that the South seceded for one reason and one reason only: to "render our liberties and institutions more secure" by "rescuing, restoring, and re-establishing the Constitution." As for the War, the South took up arms, he often noted, for no other reason than a "desire to preserve constitutional liberty and perpetuate the government in its purity."

According to the South's highest ranking military officer, General Robert E. Lee:

> All the South has ever desired was that the Union as established by our forefathers should be preserved; and that the government as originally organized should be administered in purity and truth.

From its own point of view, the North held the exact same sentiments.

No Northerner was more definitive about the true purpose, and thus the cause, of the "Civil War" than the man who started it: U.S. President Abraham Lincoln. In his Inaugural Address, March 4, 1861, only four weeks before the conflict, he declared:

> I have no purpose, directly or indirectly, to interfere with the institution of slavery in the States where it exists.

In the Summer of 1861, with the War now in full swing, he told Reverend Charles E. Lester:

> I think [Massachusetts Senator Charles] Sumner, and the rest of you [abolitionists], would upset our apple-cart altogether, if you had your way. . . . We didn't go into the war to put down Slavery, but to put the flag back . . .

On August 22, 1862, Lincoln sent this public comment to Horace Greeley, owner of the New York *Tribune*:

> My paramount object in this struggle is to save the Union, and it is not either to save or destroy slavery. If I could save the Union without freeing any slave, I would do it . . .

Impatient over misunderstandings on the topic, on August 15, 1864, Lincoln clarified his position yet again:

> My enemies pretend I am now carrying on this war for the sole purpose of abolition. So long as I am President, it shall be carried on for the sole purpose of restoring the Union.

And let us not forget Lincoln's support of the Corwin Amendment (mentioned in his First Inaugural Address), which would have guaranteed the states the right to practice slavery in perpetuity.

The U.S. Congress also testified that the Civil War had no connection to slavery. On July 22, 1861, it issued the following resolution:

> . . . this war is not waged upon our part in any spirit of oppression, nor for any purpose of conquest or subjugation, nor purpose of overthrowing or interfering with the rights or established institutions [that is, slavery] of those States; but to defend and maintain the supremacy of the Constitution and to preserve the Union with all the dignity, equality, and rights of the several States unimpaired; that as soon as these objects are accomplished the war ought to cease.

The North's most famous general, Ulysses S. Grant, made this comment on the topic of slavery and the cause of the War:

> The sole object of this war is to restore the union. Should I be convinced it has any other object, or that the government designs using its soldiers to execute the wishes of the Abolitionists, I pledge to you my honor as a man and a soldier, I would resign my commission and carry my sword to the other side.[21]

The always perspicacious Jefferson Davis summarized Lincoln's "Civil War" this way:

> . . . the war was, on the part of the United States Government, one of aggression and usurpation, and, on the part of the South, was for the defense of an inherent, unalienable right.

What was that right? The right of state sovereignty and self-determination as laid out in the Declaration of Independence, the Articles of Confederation, the Bill of Rights, and the Constitution itself (see the Ninth and Tenth Amendments in particular).[22]

FACT 16

THE NORTH DOESN'T WANT YOU TO KNOW THAT LINCOLN WAGED WAR ON THE SOUTHERN CONFEDERACY IN ORDER TO INSTALL BIG GOVERNMENT AT WASHINGTON

Why did the North fight the War then if not over slavery? Lincoln claimed it was to "preserve the Union." But this was just a smokescreen to conceal his true Liberal agenda: to install big government, then known as the "American System," in Washington.

Devised and promoted by Lincoln's political hero, slave owner Henry Clay—a man "Honest Abe" called "my *beau ideal* of a statesman, the man for whom I fought all my humble life"—the American System was a nationalist program in which there was to be a single sovereign authority, the president, who was to assume the role of a kinglike ruler with autocratic powers.

Likewise, the government at Washington, D.C. was to be federated, acting as a consolidated superpower that would eventually control the money supply, offer internal improvements, intervene in foreign affairs, nationalize the banking system, issue soaring tariffs, grant subsidies to corporations, engage in protectionism, and impose an income tax, all hints of Lincoln's coming empire.

In essence, what the American System proposed was a federated government that was the polar opposite of a confederated government. Under federation, its proponents, the Federalists, Monarchists, or Hamiltonians (named after Liberal Alexander Hamilton), as they were variously called, not only sought to create a large, domineering, all-powerful, nationalized government to which all interests (from private to business) were subordinate, but they also proposed that the states be largely stripped of their independence and authority, then placed in an inferior role. Hamilton himself wanted to get rid of the states altogether. Jeffersonianism was to be abolished and replaced with the Hamiltonian or American System.[23]

As such, nation-building nationalist Lincoln must be considered nothing less than the "Great Federator": the creator of American big government for big business, with its big spending, Big Brother mind-set. He is also either fully or partially responsible for the following: America's internal revenue program (the IRS), American protectionism, American imperialism, American expansionism, America's bloated military despotism, America's enormous standing army, America's central banking system, America's corporate welfare system (which he called "internal improvements"), America's nation-building agenda, and America's deeply entangled foreign alliances. (Lincoln apparently never read Jefferson's admonition that America's approach to foreign affairs should be: "Peace, commerce, and honest friendship with all nations, entangling alliances with none.")

Liberal Lincoln has always been revered by dictators and socialists, one of the more famous being Nazi leader Adolf Hitler.

Is it any wonder that anti-Confederacy Lincoln surrounded himself with Marxists; that he was supported by a group of radical socialists called the "Forty-Eighters"; that he was adored by nationalists, dictators, and communists from around the world, including socialists like Adolf Hitler and Francis Bellamy (author of America's *Pledge of Allegiance*); that in the 1930s American communists formed a military organization called "The Abraham Lincoln Battalion"; or that the 1939 Communist Party Convention in Chicago, Illinois, affectionately displayed an enormous image of Lincoln over the center of its stage, flanked by pictures of Russian communist dictators Vladimir Lenin on one side and Joseph Stalin on the other?

And here, politically at least, is Lincoln's greatest legacy, for big government opened the door to federal tyranny and its many dangers and horrors: the consolidation of governmental powers, the centralization of executive power, unchecked presidential power, expansion of the military, the growth of the nanny state, unlimited abuses and corruption, and the progressive, intrusive, oppressive, tax-and-spend government that American citizens now labor under, whether they are Lincolnian Liberals themselves, or Independent, Conservative, or Libertarian.

And all of this came at the expense of individual civil liberties and states' rights, the very rights our colonial and Confederate ancestors fought and died for.²⁴

The Great Yankee Coverup tells us that "Southern slaves were locked in lifelong indentures, unable to escape their brutish lives under the iron fists of their violent racist white owners." This sounds impossibly absurd—because it is! So beloved were Southern servants that not only were they treated like members of their owners' family, but when needed, white communities often banded together to raise the money to purchase and free them. One of the more renowned Southern emancipations of this type was that which concerned a Mississippi slave nicknamed the "Prince of Slaves," or "Prince" for short. In his previous life Prince had been a high-ranking member of the Timbo people in Africa, where his name had been Abdul Rahman Ibrahim Ibn Sori. Though he was the son of a Timbo king, he had been captured—as was the African custom—by fellow Africans during a local war and enslaved. In Prince's case, however, he was later bartered to Yankee slave traders, after which he was transported to America and fortunately sold South. In the early 1800s he pleaded his case for freedom. Kentucky slaveholder Henry Clay and many others came to Prince's defense, and eventually his kindly owner freed him at great financial loss. When it was discovered that Prince's wife was still enslaved, the white citizens of Natchez, Mississippi, generously raised the funds for her purchase as well, with additional money for a "flowing Moorish costume in which Prince was promptly arrayed." In 1828 the couple sailed off to Morocco, all expenses paid.

FACT 17

THE NORTH DOESN'T WANT YOU TO KNOW THAT THE AMERICAN CIVIL WAR WAS A CONSERVATIVE VS. LIBERAL CONFLICT

The "Civil War" then did not concern slavery. Rather as Confederate Vice President Alexander H. Stephens and others repeatedly noted, it was a battle between what were then called "Consolidationists" or "Centralists" (that is, Liberals who wanted to consolidate all power in the central government) and "Federalists" or "Constitutionalists" (that is, Conservatives who wanted to maintain states' rights and the constitutional separation of powers).

Alexander H. Stephens correctly defined the "Civil War" as a conflict between conservative "Constitutionalists" and liberal "Consolidationists."

In essence the Civil War was a battle between Southern agrarianism and Northern industrialism; between the farming and commerce capitalism of the South and the finance and industry capitalism of the North; between Southern free trade and Northern protective tariffs; between Southern traditionalism and Northern progressivism; between Southern ruralism (the countryman) and Northern urbanism (the townsman); between Southern conservatism and Northern liberalism; between the South's desire to maintain Thomas Jefferson's "Confederate Republic" and the North's desire to change it into Alexander Hamilton's federate democracy.

Shorn of Northern myth and anti-South propaganda, Lincoln's War was nothing but a conflict that pitted liberal, progressive, Northern industrialists who cared little for the Constitution, against conservative, traditional, Southern agriculturalists who were strict constitutionalists.[25]

As we are all well aware, this Liberal vs. Conservative conflict still rages on today, just as potently as it did in the 1860s.[26]

FACT 18

THE NORTH DOESN'T WANT YOU TO KNOW THAT IT WAS NOT THE SOUTH THAT LOST THE CIVIL WAR, IT WAS AMERICA

As we have seen, one of dictator Lincoln's major goals was to install the socialistic American System at Washington. This could not be done, however, with the constitutional guarantee of states' rights in place, so the Constitution needed to be overthrown. The Constitution-loving South was not about to allow this to occur, a sentiment it had been voicing for decades. The Southern states' answer to Lincoln's plan was to simply secede quietly and peacefully before he began dismantling the Constitution—their attempt to retain the original U.S. Constitution by forming a second Confederate States of America in imitation of the first. This is why Southern secession began in December 1860, *after*, not before, Lincoln's election.

In April 1861, by which time Lincoln realized that the exit of the Southern states would impede his dream of big government, he called for 75,000 troops to invade Dixie, a hurried effort to crush the states' rights movement in the South before it grew any larger. Technically speaking though, it was not the South he was going to war against. It was what the South represented, and that was and still is the number one objective of the Conservative Party: preservation of the Constitution, with its tacit guarantee of state home rule or self-government.

Though because of The Great Yankee Coverup this fact is virtually unknown today, it was very familiar to both the average Confederate soldier and his superiors. Thus in 1900 one of the latter, Confederate General Stephen Dill Lee, a cousin of mine and of General Robert E. Lee, said unequivocally of the Southern Cause:

> We men of the South made as gallant a struggle as was ever made *for constitutional principles.* Upon the fields of battle the boys in gray fought with valor for *a great cause* . . .[27]

In 1919, Georgia's state historian emeritus, Lucian Lamar Knight, made a similar but even clearer statement on this topic:

> [When the South] drew her sword against the Union's flag, *it was in defence of the Union's Constitution!* . . . Nor was it African slavery for which the South contended, but Anglo-Saxon freedom—the old Teutonic birthright of *self-government and home rule!*[28]

Even most foreigners were aware of the truth about the War and Lincoln's intentions to trample the Constitution and economically conquer, plunder, and control the South under the guise of "abolition." In 1861 one of them, famed English novelist Charles Dickens, wrote:

> *The Northern onslaught upon slavery is no more than a piece of specious humbug disguised to conceal its desire for economic control of the United States.* Union means so many millions a year lost to the South; secession means loss of the same millions to the North. The love of money is the root of this as many, many other evils. *The quarrel between the North and South is, as it stands, solely a fiscal quarrel.*[29]

In short, the South sought to maintain the Constitution by seceding from the North, while the North sought to overturn it by subduing the South.

The Yankees' fiendish plans included their so-called "Civil War Amendments," the Thirteenth, Fourteenth, and Fifteenth Amendments: after the War all three were used by the Liberal North to strip sovereign power from the states and transfer it to the Federal government. The Civil War Amendments had little to do with black civil rights, as Liberals continue to maintain to this day. They were only conceived to masquerade as such. In fact, they were anti-South, and thus anti-Conservative, anti-states' rights amendments, plain and simple, a fact that has been recognized by Southerners ever

Until the end of his life Confederate General Stephen Dill Lee maintained what every traditional Southerner still knows to be true: the South fought, not to "keep slavery" or "destroy the Union," but for a "great cause"; namely, the preservation of the original U.S. Constitution. Thus, as the author notes, the South's loss was actually America's loss.

since they were ratified between 1865 and 1870.

It is evident that Lincoln and his Northern constituents intentionally, and with malice aforethought, denigrated and eroded America's longstanding laws and traditions by illegitimately initiating a war, subverting the Constitution, curtailing civil liberties, illegally invading a sovereign nation (the CSA), meddling in foreign affairs, despoiling that nation's land, destroying her infrastructure, unlawfully redistributing Southern land and wealth (one of Lincoln's many socialistic programs), and maiming, imprisoning, torturing, starving, raping, and killing as many as 2 million of Dixie's people. All for what purpose? To realize Liberal Lincoln's enigmatical obsession with big government and "preserving the Union," a union that its very founders based on small government and the right of secession—and which they purposefully designed to be impermanent, malleable, open, and voluntary. Our American *führer*, the Naziesque Abraham Lincoln, changed all that on April 9, 1865, with Lee's surrender at Appomattox, Virginia, making the Union permanent, inflexible, closed, and involuntary.[30]

It is nothing but a Yankee lie that "the South lost the Civil War." In reality, it was a national tragedy that has negatively impacted every aspect of American life to this day.

The North may have won, but this only proved that she had the money and military might to force her opinion on the South, not that she was in the right. Indeed, it is obvious to all thinking people that the North was dead wrong. To put it another way, "the South was right," just as Confederate champion John A. Richardson declared in 1914. This is why, to this day, the South's fight to save the constitutional (Confederate) government of the Founding generation continues among the Southern Confederacy's modern political descendants: today's Conservative and Libertarian Parties, the contemporary extensions of Old South constitutionalism.

There is good reason why I call the Civil War "Lincoln's War on the Constitution and the American People" ("Lincoln's War" for short). For it was not the South, but America which lost the "Civil War," and every American—Southerner, Northerner, Easterner, or Westerner—is today the poorer for it.[31]

FACT 19

THE NORTH DOESN'T WANT YOU TO KNOW THAT THE CONFEDERACY ENLISTED BLACK SOLDIERS LONG BEFORE THE UNION DID

The South's first all-black militia was officially formed on April 23, 1861, only nine days after the first battle of the War at Fort Sumter, South Carolina. The unit, known as the "Native Guards (colored)," was "duly and legally enrolled as a part of the militia of the State, its officers being commissioned by Thomas O. Moore, Governor and Commander-in-Chief of the State of Louisiana . . ."

In contrast, the North's first all-black militia, the First South Carolina Volunteers, was not commissioned until over a year and a half later (on November 7, 1862), under Yankee Colonel Thomas Wentworth Higginson.

Indeed, Lincoln did not allow *official* black enlistment until January 1, 1863, with the issuance of his Final Emancipation Proclamation, as that document tacitly states. Up until then he had strictly barred both blacks and Native-Americans (whom he and his administration referred to as "savages") from joining the Union military as armed soldiers.

It was not the North, but the South—under Louisiana Governor Thomas O. Moore—that first officially enlisted blacks in its military.

Since blacks had served officially, legally, and courageously as soldiers in *all* of America's conflicts up until the Civil War, Lincoln must be named as the one who injected white racism and racial segregation into the U.S. military for the first time, an unfortunate situation that lasted well into the late 1940s.[32]

FACT 20

THE NORTH DOESN'T WANT YOU TO KNOW THAT AS MANY AS 1 MILLION AFRICAN-AMERICANS FOUGHT FOR THE CONFEDERACY

The truth that you will never read in pro-North Civil War histories is that far more blacks fought for the Confederacy than for the Union. The Union possessed about 3 million soldiers. Of these about 200,000 were black, 6 percent of the total. The Confederacy had about 1 million soldiers. Of these an estimated 300,000 were black, 30 percent of the total. Simply put: 30 percent of Davis' army was black, but only 6 percent of Lincoln's army was black.

And these numbers are conservative if we use the definition of a "private soldier" as determined by German-American Union General August Valentine Kautz in 1864:

> In the fullest sense, any man in the military service who receives pay, whether sworn in or not, is a soldier, because he is subject to military law. Under this general head, laborers, teamsters, sutlers, chaplains, etc., are soldiers.

By Kautz's definition of a "private soldier," some 2 million Southerners fought for the Confederacy: 1 million whites and perhaps as many as 1 million blacks.

As most of the 4 million blacks (3.5 million servants, 500,000 free) living in the South at the time of Lincoln's War remained loyal to the Confederacy, and as at least 1 million of these either worked in or fought in the Rebel army and navy in some capacity, Kautz' definition raises the percentage of Southern blacks who defended the Confederacy as real soldiers to as much as 50 percent of the total Confederate soldier population—five times or 500 percent more than fought for the Union.[33]

FACT 21

THE NORTH DOESN'T WANT YOU TO KNOW THAT THE NORTHERN ARMIES WERE RACIALLY SEGREGATED, WHILE THE SOUTHERN ARMIES WERE RACIALLY INTEGRATED

Lincoln not only stalled official black enlistment in the U.S. army, but when he finally allowed it he imposed strict racist policies on his African-American soldiers, including segregation and unequal pay.

Lincoln, a dyed-in-the-wool white separatist, was literally obsessed with the idea of American apartheid (the geographical segregation of the races), which is one reason why, when he was a member of the Illinois legislature, he asked for funds to expel all free blacks from the state. This was also the reason he became a manager of the Illinois chapter of the American Colonization Society, which one day hoped to make the entire U.S. "as white as New England."

Not surprisingly, after finally allowing official black enlistment in 1863, Lincoln ordered all of his black troops to be racially segregated, led by white officers, and paid half that of white enlistees, infuriating both his black soldiery and Northern abolitionists.

Naturally, in the far more racially tolerant South, birthplace of the American abolition movement, President Davis simply integrated blacks directly into his army and navy. As in Southern society itself, there was no desire for segregation among the South's military forces. For unlike in the racist North, Southern troops neither wanted segregation or needed it.[34]

FACT 22

THE NORTH DOESN'T WANT YOU TO KNOW THAT THANKS TO LINCOLN THE UNION ARMY WAS THE MOST RACIST MILITARY IN AMERICAN HISTORY

To begin with, white Yankee soldiers were well-known for their racial bigotry and utter intolerance of blacks. This is just one of the many reasons Lincoln would not permit blacks to serve as active combatants in the U.S. military during the first half of his War. As hesitant Lincoln put it to a group of abolitionist clergyman on September 13, 1862, a few days prior to issuing his Preliminary Emancipation Proclamation:

> . . . I am not so sure we could do much with the blacks. If we were to arm them, I fear that in a few weeks the arms would be in the hands of the rebels; and, indeed, thus far we have not had arms enough to equip our white troops.

Lincoln's hesitation was warranted, but not for the reason he states: when he finally allowed full-fledged black recruitment, white soldiers hissed and booed, desertions increased, and a general "demoralization" set in across the entire Federal military.

The mere mention of the idea of "black enlistment" brought many white regiments close to insurrection. A Yankee soldier with the 90th Illinois reported on the general feeling among his fellow Union compatriots at the time: "Not one of our boys wants to give guns to the Negroes. This is a white man's war and that's the way we want to keep it. Besides we have no desire to fight next to blacks on the battlefield," he asserted.

Northern white outrage at the idea of enlisting blacks was somewhat mitigated when Lincoln ordered the army and navy to be racially segregated, but newly recruited blacks were not happy with the president's command that all colored troops were to be officered by whites. Even pro-North historians have had to concede that white Northern soldiers were "bitterly hostile . . . to Negro troops."

White Yankee racism continued well into the War. During inclement weather, for example, white Yankee soldiers were known to beat black Yankee soldiers, then push them out into the freezing night air in order to have the tents all to themselves.

Most white Union officers never completely accepted commanding black troops, as there was "no prestige" in it. In fact so few white officers could be found who were willing to "lower" themselves to leading blacks that white privates, induced with the promise of promotion, finally had to be virtually coerced into taking the positions.

The situation got so out of hand that Federal officers had to be ordered to "treat black soldiers as soldiers," and the word "nigger," along with degrading disciplinary action and routine offensive language aimed at blacks, had to be banned with harsh punishments. Meanwhile white Union soldiers continued to put on minstrel shows that satirized and humiliated African-Americans, a not uncommon form of entertainment, particularly on Yankee warships.

But Northern white racism in the U.S. army often manifested in far more serious and diabolical ways. Southern diaries, letters, and journals are replete with reports of incredible Yankee brutality against not only white Southern women they came across, but black Southern women as well, even against those that had at first cheered them on as liberators. Yankee soldiers' crimes against black females included robbery, pillage, beatings, torture, rape, and even murder.

Southern black males were often treated even worse by their Northern "emancipators." Those who survived such crimes were taken, against their will at gunpoint, from their relatively peaceful, healthy, and safe lives of service and domesticity on the plantation, to the filth, hardships, and dangers of life on the battlefield, where at least 50 percent of them died alone in muddy ditches fighting for the Yanks against their own native land: the South.

Those blacks who resisted "involuntary enlistment" into Lincoln's army were sometimes shot or bayoneted on the spot. When black soldiers rebelled against the abuse of white Yankee soldiers, they were whipped. Both white and black Union soldiers were known to abuse Southern slaves who remained loyal to Dixie, entering their homes, shooting bullets through the walls, overturning furniture, and stealing various personal items.

Is this appalling? Not when we realize that this was all merely a continuation of Lincoln's policy of coercion, the same one he had used to invade the South in an attempt to destroy states' rights to begin with.

Many newly "freed" black males were used as Yankee shock troops, sent first into battle in conflicts usually known beforehand to be hopeless, where they would draw fire and take the brunt of the violence, sparing the lives of Northern whites. This is almost certainly what Lincoln was intimating in his letter to James C. Conkling on August 26, 1863, when he wrote:

> . . . whatever negroes can be got to do as soldiers, leaves just so much less for white soldiers to do in saving the Union.

This included, of course, receiving cold Confederate steel.

Blacks who were finally allowed to enlist in the Union army by their reluctant president, however, were in for a rude surprise if they expected to don a fancy new uniform and fight next to whites on the battlefield. For at the beginning of black enlistment, Lincoln turned nearly all freed black males into common workers who performed what can only be described as "forced labor"; in other words, slavery. Their work, in fact, was identical to the drudgery they had experienced as slaves. Black military duties under Lincoln included construction, serving officers (known in the South as "body servants"), cooking, washing clothes and dishes, tending livestock, and cleaning stables.

Actually, the first black soldiers in the U.S. military were not allowed to serve as active combatants in any form; rather they were signed up specifically to work as ordinary grunts: teamsters, blacksmiths, carpenters, masons, scouts, longshoremen, pioneers, wheelwrights, medical assistants, orderlies, laundry workers, spies, and of course, "slaves," almost anything but armed fighters. Most were to be used merely for monotonous guard duty, or as Lincoln himself put it in his Final Emancipation Proclamation,

> to garrison forts, positions, stations, and other places, and to man vessels of all sorts in said service.[35]

FACT 23

THE NORTH DOESN'T WANT YOU TO KNOW HOW MANY SOUTHERNERS WERE ACTUALLY KILLED DURING LINCOLN'S WAR

Pro-North writers have long claimed that only 329,000 Confederate soldiers died during the Civil War, hardly what one would call a bloodbath compared to the millions that died during conflicts like World War II.

Yet, this is a purely Northern figure, and as such inaccurate. For one thing it completely disregards the many thousands of Southern noncombatants who perished, such as European-American seniors, women, and children. It also does not include free Southern African-Americans or black servants (men, women, and children).

The practice of omitting these losses from the total has long been employed by Yankee and scallywag historians to artificially keep down the number of Southern dead. For if the true number were known to the public, even greater justification would be needed for Lincoln's War, far beyond the obvious lies that have been created for it thus far.

According to we traditional Southern historians, an estimated 2 million Southerners died during Lincoln's War: 1 million whites (out of 8 million) and probably as many as 1 million blacks (out of 4 million). This is a stunning 16 percent of Dixie's total white and black population (of 12 million). There is no record of how many Southern Asians, Native-Americans, and Hispanics also died in the conflict, but we can be sure these deaths easily numbered in the many thousands. In short, 12.5 percent of all Southern whites died, while 25 percent of all Southern blacks died as a direct result of Lincoln and his War.

The number of dead on the Union side we put at 1 million, which means that in all (South and North combined) some 3 million died as a direct result of Lincoln and his War, 10 percent of the total American population of 30 million at the time. This is what we Southerners call a bloodbath.

Let us note here that this is the modern equivalent of our current president killing 30 million Americans (10 percent of our present day population of 300 million) for leaving the union peacefully, legally, and constitutionally. Would we revere him, annually vote him our "favorite president," and carve his visage into Mount Rushmore? Would we emblazon his face on our penny, our five dollar bill, and the Illinois license plate? Would we name schools, businesses, organizations, streets, towns, and counties, and even our children, after him?

No. He would be arrested, tried, convicted, and put to death for war crimes, his name and legacy forever blackened in the pages of history.

Though Lincoln was in fact responsible for the deaths of the modern day equivalent of 30 million Americans—more people than were killed by Joseph Stalin (12 million) and Adolf Hitler (16 million) combined—"Honest Abe" continues to be apotheosized, idolized, and worshiped like a Pagan god. Little wonder that the uneducated gave him his own paganesque "temple" in Washington, D.C., one that makes the ancient temples of Jupiter and Zeus pale by comparison.[36]

We in the South say this is wrong. Yankees, what say you?

According to The Great Yankee Coverup, only 110,000 Union soldiers and 329,000 Confederate soldiers were killed during Lincoln's War, a combined sum of 439,000. Southern historians, however, have estimated that at least 3 million died in total, the equivalent of 30 million Americans (or ten percent of 300 million) today.

FACT 24

THE NORTH DOESN'T WANT YOU TO KNOW THAT THE WAR WAS UNNECESSARY & AVOIDABLE

The truth is that no conflict was ever more unnecessary and avoidable than Lincoln's War. Not only was secession legal, but the Yankee president did not preserve the *voluntary* union created by the Founding Fathers, nor did he end slavery, which was only finally abolished eight months after he died under the Thirteenth Amendment.

Of course, the War was not about slavery to begin with; and regardless, ending slavery was not one of Lincoln's original goals to begin with, as he himself stated in his First Inaugural Address. As mentioned, our sixteenth chief executive may have been mentally unstable, but he was not unintelligent: freeing the slaves then compensating Southern slave owners for their financial losses would have cost the U.S. ten times less than what it cost to go to war.

Even if the War had been about slavery, the South, the birthplace of the American abolition movement, had been working on plans for complete emancipation since the 1600s, making the conflict, from any viewpoint, absolutely unnecessary.

We Southerners are all too familiar with Yankee William H. Seward's monstrous fable that the War was an "irrepressible conflict," for pro-North historians have forced this phrase into all of our textbooks and history books. What they conveniently leave out is the fact that Lincoln's secretary of state twisted the truth in order to justify Lincoln's many crimes against the South, against the Northern people, and against the Constitution.

The South only wanted peace and, before the War, did everything in her power to maintain it. As threats of violence began to come from Washington, D.C. in early 1861, Confederate President Jefferson Davis sent one peace commission after another to the U.S. White House in an attempt to prevent bloodshed. During the War he did everything in his power to draw the conflict to a close as soon as possible.

Lincoln, in contrast, actively sought war, created one illegally, and then sustained it for as long as possible, all in pursuit of his personal liberal agenda: big government, a national bank, protectionism, and government subsidies (which he called "internal improvements"). Along the way he spurned all attempts, both by his cabinet members and by his Northern constituents, to end the War and allow the South to go her own way in peace. Had differences been settled legally in court, or at least diplomatically—as they should have been, and as the South repeatedly tried to do, the entire tragedy could have easily been prevented.

The "Civil War" was not irresistible, inevitable, or "America's destiny," as many Northerners saw it—and still see it. This is just another Yankee folktale designed to help prop up The Great Yankee Coverup.[37]

The War was only "irrepressible" to Abraham Lincoln, and this is because he wanted war. In the more peace-loving South Jefferson Davis sent ongoing peace commissions to Washington, both before and during the War, in an effort to halt the bloodshed. But Lincoln refused to meet with any Confederate diplomats until February 1865, by which point he knew that the Union would be victorious.

FACT 25

THE NORTH DOESN'T WANT YOU TO KNOW WHY THE SOUTH WILL NEVER STOP FIGHTING FOR THE PRINCIPLES UNDERLYING THE CIVIL WAR

There is a common refrain in the North: Why are Southerners still fighting the Civil War? Why can't they accept that they lost and move on?

The South is indeed still fighting. But it is not the "Civil War." She is still fighting for the principles and ideas that her ancestors died for in that conflict to begin with; namely, strict constitutionality, states' rights, a small limited central government, conservative Jeffersonian political ideals, free trade, capitalism, fiscal responsibility, and traditional family and religious values.

All of these are being slowly eroded and replaced by the liberal, nationalistic, industry-based, Hamiltonian, big-government-loving, Federalist North, a process leftover from Lincoln's Reconstruction campaign to destroy the Old South and Northernize her by remaking her in the image of the northeastern states—the last thing any red-blooded Southerner would ever want. Thus the South fights on. Not the War itself, but for the ideals over which her ancestors fought and perished.

In point of fact it would be more accurate to say that it is the North who is still fighting the War. Each year thousands of books, articles, films, and blogs are produced on Lincoln's War, nearly all of them slanted toward the Northern perspective; nearly every one overflowing with Yankee mythology, lies, slander, misinformation, and disinformation; nearly every one created by politically correct non-Southerners and (traitorous) New South Southerners, both who are ignorant of our true history, and who thus misunderstand and revile Dixie. Yet when a Southerner attempts to defend his homeland and heritage against this avalanche of ludicrous and often purposefully hurtful fiction, he or she is reprimanded for "still fighting the Civil War." It is just another cog in the machinery of The Great Yankee Coverup.[38]

FACT 26

THE NORTH DOESN'T WANT YOU TO KNOW THAT THE SOUTHERN CONFEDERACY & ITS GOVERNMENT ARE BOTH STILL ALIVE & WELL

The North teaches that the Southern Confederacy was an illegitimate and therefore unauthorized and fictitious government, and that its surrender to the Union on April 9, 1865, marked its official end. We have already seen that the first charge is false, for the Confederacy was, without question, a constitutionally formed legal republic.

Only the Confederate Congress had the power to shut down the government of the Confederate States of America, and this it never did.

As for the second accusation, it is true that Confederate General Robert. E. Lee signed Union General Ulysses S. Grant's "surrender agreement." But even though he was the highest ranking Rebel military officer at the time, Lee lacked the authority to make such a momentous political decision. The Confederate Congress, the only body with such power, never signed a single sheet of paper authorizing the termination of the Confederate government, the permanent suspension of the Confederate Constitution, or the dissolution of the Confederate States.

All are technically still intact and active, awaiting the right time and the right individuals to relaunch what St. George Tucker called the "Confederate Republic," what Thomas Jefferson referred to as "a lasting Confederacy," and what Alexis de Tocqueville called the "confederate states of America": the government originally intended by the U.S. Founding Fathers.[39]

FACT 27

THE NORTH DOESN'T WANT YOU TO KNOW THAT MORE CONFEDERATE PRISONERS DIED IN YANKEE PRISONS THAN YANKEE PRISONERS IN CONFEDERATE PRISONS

Newly captured Confederate soldiers, Gettysburg, July 1863.

The Great Yankee Coverup teaches that Union prisons were nowhere near as bad as Confederate prisons. This statement would have been deeply disturbing to most traditional 19th-Century Southerners, particularly the nearly 6,000 Confederate prisoners who were tortured then purposefully starved to death by Yankee Colonel Benjamin J. Sweet at Chicago's notorious Camp Douglas—a Yankee prison rightly referred to by all who witnessed it as "Eighty Acres of Hell."

Numerous other such places could be named, such as the Yankees' Johnson's Island Prison, known as the "Northern Andersonville"; Lincoln's gulag, the barbaric and horribly overcrowded Fort Lafayette in New York Harbor; and the New York Federal garrison called Elmira Prison (or "Hellmira," as inmates referred to it), where nearly 3,000 Confederates died unnecessarily. Is it any wonder that Rebel prisoners believed they had a better chance of surviving on the battlefield?

The truth of the matter, as Lincoln's own Secretary of War Edwin M. Stanton noted, is that a higher percentage of Southern POWs perished in Yankee prisons than Northern POWs in Confederate prisons. Some estimate the Rebel prisoner loss to be as high as 200,000, while the Yankee prisoner loss was only between 23,000 and 30,000.

As hard as anti-South, pro-North historians try, no amount of whitewashing American history or brainwashing the American public can change these facts.[40]

FACT 28

THE NORTH DOESN'T WANT YOU TO KNOW THAT THE SOUTH WOULD HAVE WON THE WAR HAD IT FOUGHT FOR JUST ONE MORE YEAR

Anti-South historians would like you to believe that because the North had three times the manpower and three times the supplies, that it could have continued the War forever, and that the arrest of Jefferson Davis on May 10, 1865, finally killed off the last vestige of "rebelliousness" in Dixie.

The truth is that, according to none other than Yankee General Ulysses S. Grant, Lincoln's claim that "the contest could have been continued indefinitely" is false. In his 1885 *Memoirs* Grant revealed that if Confederate General Nathan Bedford Forrest's protraction strategy (endorsed by numerous Rebel officers, including General Joseph E. Johnston) had been adopted by the South, the Confederacy would have won the War within one year. (Forrest's brilliant plan called for prolonging the conflict—thus exhausting the North—by closing down the Yankees' major supply routes, the Mississippi and Tennessee Rivers).[41] Wrote Grant:

Cigar-chomping Union General Ulysses S. Grant.

> I think that [this] . . . policy was the best one that could have been pursued by the whole South—protract the war, which was all that was necessary to enable them to gain recognition in the end. The North was already growing weary . . . Anything that could have prolonged the war a year beyond the time that it did finally close, would probably have exhausted the North to such an extent that they might then have abandoned the contest and agreed to separation.

It is clear now why the ingenious Jefferson Davis wanted to continue the War, even after Lee's "surrender."[42]

FACT 29

THE NORTH DOESN'T WANT YOU TO KNOW THAT THE OLD SOUTH & THE OLD NORTH WERE INCOMPATIBLE FROM THE BEGINNING

Pro-North writers, and Liberals in general, delight in portraying the Old North and the Old South as two nearly identical regions, socially, politically, and spiritually. Originally, the idea behind this view, one still being advanced by Northern propagandists, was that 19th-Century America was "one big happy family," making the South's secession not just "treasonous," but an anti-social act of "rebellion" against her loving and respectful "brothers and sisters" to the North.

As with all aspects of The Great Yankee Coverup, this one too is false, and there is plenty of evidence to substantiate the fact.

In the mid 1800s no two parts of the U.S. were more unalike than the South and the North. The patent distinctions between the CSA and the USA actually have ancient roots, profound dissimilarities that long predate even the birth of America in 1776.

Already in that year the two regions were manifesting sharp cultural, religious, social, and political differences. They were like two separate nations, two nations that many believe (myself among them) would have been better off not uniting to begin with. Indeed, their differences only became more evident when the Southern and the Northern colonies combined, forming Jefferson's American Confederacy in 1781, later to be known as the United States of America. Southern historian Frank Lawrence Owsley rightly saw this merger as the union of two completely different business and societal models, two opposing civilizations, in fact.

Far from the Yankee myth that the South and North were equals, homogenous, compatible, even interchangeable, the two were actually separated by a deep cultural chasm that few today, particularly in the North, appreciate. Many modern Southerners too, now accustomed to Northern accents (thanks to the contemporary "Second Yankee Invasion") of the South) have forgotten how divergent the two regions once were.

Prior to the "Civil War" the North was primarily industrial, institutional, urban, nationalistic, liberal, radical, conformist, agnostic, Catholic, progressive, business oriented, and publicly schooled. To the Yankee mind the Union was a purely commercial entity, a single monolithic democracy by which that region could profit through tariffs, bounties, and "sectional aggrandizement."

In contrast to this worldview, known as "Yankeeism" in the South, Dixie was mainly agricultural, personal, rural, localistic, conservative, Constitutional, individualistic, intensely religious, Protestant, traditional, family oriented, and home-schooled. To the Southern mind the Union was a moral social order, a "friendly association" of states held together by "good faith," the "exchanges of equity and comity," and the concept of states' rights.

There were a number of other social and cultural differences, as well. As the South saw it, Northerners were discourteous and reserved, while they themselves were well mannered and emotional. Northerners were greedy, shrewd, and materialistic, while Southerners were generous, hospitable, and spiritual. Northern society was prim, proper, and fast-paced, Southern society was relaxed, informal, and leisurely.

Pro tempore president of South Carolina's secession convention, David F. Jamison, spoke for most Southerners when, in 1861, he referred to what he saw as the "jealousy," "aggressions," "cupidity," and "avarice of the Northern people . . ." Tired of Yankee meddling, overtaxation, and annoying insults, and violently resenting the North's constant attempt to interfere with the South's local and state affairs, Jamison lamented: "As there is no common bond between us, all attempts to continue as united will only prove futile." How true.

Could any two regions have been more culturally, politically, religiously, psychologically, spiritually, and socially opposite one another? We think not, and neither did our Southern ancestors, just one of the many reasons they decided to secede from a Union they saw as alien and even hostile to their interests.

Far from being a homogenized nation even in the mid 1800s, this great cultural divide continues to separate the two regions a century and a half after the "Civil War." The "Yankee Go Home!" bumper sticker is still one of the most popular in the South.[43]

82 ∾ THE GREAT YANKEE COVERUP

If we were to take The Great Yankee Coverup literally, we might assume that the Southern Confederacy and her beautiful Battle Flag have been detested by Northerners ever since the end of Lincoln's War, 150 years ago. But, in fact, the burning hatred of the South and her symbols that we see across the North today is actually a recent contrivance of the anti-South movement. How does it work? By portraying the South as "racist" and the North as "anti-racist," the Liberal socialistic leaders of the anti-South movement inflame racial animosity between the two regions. This fake "race war" helps them raise money to maintain their bogus "anti-racist" organizations, without which such race-baiters and race-merchants could not survive financially. As any educated socialist knows—and as socialist Hitler so cruelly demonstrated—a country weakened by conflict is much easier to put under governmental control, which is precisely the goal of these unprincipled anti-American groups. And they continue to flourish in the North, and now even in parts of the New South, despite the historical fact that since the 1700s both foreign and domestic travelers have taken great pains to point out that the white North has always been far more racist than the white South. The South-loathing crowd prefers to ignore these important eyewitness accounts. But it is more difficult to disregard photographs produced by the U.S. government. In the picture here, for example, our thirtieth president, Calvin Coolidge, hosts a Confederate group in front of the White House in December 1927. Several of the men are wearing Confederate uniforms and two are holding up Confederate Battle Flags. The president has a look of solemnity and respect in the presence of these Southern gentlemen, perfectly befitting the occasion. Thanks to the indefatigable ongoing efforts of pro-North Liberals, the public mind has been thoroughly poisoned by anti-South lies, propaganda, and slander, making it highly unlikely that this scene will ever be repeated again.

Did Lincoln "preserve the Union"? Of course not, and even many Northerners were once aware of this fact. Maryland journalist, H. L. Mencken, for example, had this to say about Lincoln's most celebrated pro-Union declamation, the Gettysburg Address: "The Gettysburg speech was at once the shortest and the most famous oration in American history. . . the highest emotion reduced to a few poetical phrases. Lincoln himself never even remotely approached it. It is genuinely stupendous. But let us not forget that it is poetry, not logic; beauty, not sense. Think of the argument in it. Put it into the cold words of everyday. The doctrine is simply this: that the Union soldiers who died at Gettysburg sacrificed their lives to the cause of self-determination—that government of the people, by the people, for the people, should not perish from the earth. It is difficult to imagine anything more untrue. The Union soldiers in the battle actually fought against self-determination; it was the Confederates who fought for the right of their people to govern themselves." The great irony of Lincoln is that during his lifetime he was voted America's worst president, and the direct cause of disunion, America's bloodiest and most expensive war, and the unnecessary deaths of thousands. He was also denounced as the leader of our nation's most corrupt and diabolical administration, and the man responsible for the loss of the Founding Father's Confederate government, the destruction of the original Constitution, increased racial strife, and the near annihilation of much of what was good, beautiful, noble, and unique about the South. Yet after death, thanks to the diligent and overly imaginative work of Lincoln hagiographers, eulogists, and mythologists, he was recast as the Nation's Healer, the Great Emancipator, the Great Peacemaker, the Great Preserver, the Greatest of all Presidents. Thanks to The Great Yankee Coverup, most will never know that even Lincoln's nickname, "Honest Abe," was not meant literally but oppositionally—in the same way that a tall man is sometimes nicknamed "Little John." In other words, it was Lincoln's appalling unscrupulous amoral behavior that earned him his most famous moniker.

SECTION THREE

RACE & SLAVERY

A Persian king accompanied by two of his thousands of slaves, an illustration that simultaneously destroys two myths of The Great Yankee Coverup. 1) Slavery is not a recent nor a purely Western development. It has existed among all known peoples, societies, and cultures, and on all continents since prehistoric times. 2) Slavery is not a racist institution, invented by whites to hurt and exploit non-whites. Persian leaders *and* their slaves, as just one example, were both Caucasian, a custom that was followed in other nations across both the Middle East and Europe for thousands of years.

FACT 30

THE NORTH DOESN'T WANT YOU TO KNOW THAT IT WAS ITS DEPENDENCE ON THE YANKEE SLAVE TRADE, NOT SOUTHERN SLAVERY, THAT HELPED LAUNCH THE CIVIL WAR

We have long been taught that the North fought the Confederacy over *Southern* slavery. At the time, however, it was *Northern* slavery that was the principle interest to Yankees. As New England abolitionist Lysander Spooner and many others have pointed out, it was the North's heavy dependence on the Yankee slave trade and on selling its slaves to the South, that both precipitated and helped the Union fund the Civil War.[44]

Massachusetts abolitionist Lysander Spooner rightly referred to Lincoln's financial backers as "lenders of blood money" for using the profits of Yankee slavery to fund the president's "Civil War" on the Constitution and the American people.

In March 1861 the newly constitutionally formed Confederate States of America adopted its Constitution, which included a clause banning slave trading with foreign nations. "Foreign nations," of course, now included the United States of America. The North panicked, deciding it was better to beat the South into submission than allow her to cut off one of her primary revenue streams: the transatlantic Yankee slave trade.

Big government Liberal Abraham Lincoln, the only 1860 presidential candidate who promised *not* to interfere with slavery, and who was put into office by Northern industrialists using profits from the Northern slave trade, launched the War of Northern Aggression in April, just a few weeks later.[45]

FACT 31

THE NORTH DOESN'T WANT YOU TO KNOW THAT THE OLD NORTH WAS FAR MORE RACIST THAN THE OLD SOUTH

Scores of eyewitness accounts, both domestic and foreign, reveal that the Old North was far more racist than the Old South. As early as 1831 individuals like French aristocrat Alexis de Tocqueville, who toured the South and the North that year, noticed that Southerners were "much more tolerant and compassionate" toward blacks than Northerners. This is why, while visiting America in the 1850s, Englishman Sir Charles Lyell observed that the Southern states justifiably "make louder professions than the Northerners of democratic principles and love of equality."

The overt racial discrepancy between the South and the North was also remarked on by British journalists, even in the middle of the Civil War. In 1862 the *North British Review* noted that in the North, "where slavers are fitted out by scores . . . free Negroes are treated like lepers." This was the same year Union President Abraham Lincoln issued his Preliminary Emancipation Proclamation, which, of course, called for continued efforts to deport all freed blacks out of the U.S.

After his travels across the U.S. in 1831 and 1832, Tocqueville summed up his observations this way:

> Whosoever has inhabited the United States must have perceived that in those parts of the Union in which the negroes are no longer slaves, they have in no wise drawn nearer to the whites. On the contrary, the prejudice of the race appears to be stronger in the States which have abolished slavery than in those where it still exists; and nowhere is it so intolerant as in those States where servitude never has been known.

In the 1840s, English writer James Silk Buckingham wrote that "the prejudice of colour is not nearly so strong in the South as in the

North." Here is how Robert Young Hayne, a South Carolina senator, described the treatment of those few Southern blacks who fled to the North:

> . . . there does not exist on the face of the whole earth, a population so poor, so wretched, so vile, so loathsome, so utterly destitute of all the comforts, conveniences, and decencies of life, as the unfortunate blacks of Philadelphia, and New York and Boston. Liberty has been to them the greatest of calamities, the heaviest of curses. Sir, I have had some opportunities of making comparison between the condition of the free negroes of the North, and the slaves of the South, and the comparison has left not only an indelible impression of the superior advantages of the latter, but has gone far to reconcile me to slavery itself. Never have I felt so forcibly that touching description, 'the foxes have holes, and the birds of the air have nests, but the Son of Man hath not where to lay his head,' as when I have seen this unhappy race, naked and houseless, almost starving in the streets, and abandoned by all the world. Sir, I have seen, in the neighborhood of one of the most moral, religious and refined cities of the North, a family of free blacks driven to the caves of the rocks, and there obtaining a precarious subsistence from charity and plunder.

Only a few years later, in 1835, Virginian James Madison met with English author Harriet Martineau and regaled her with stories about how the Northern states erected numerous barriers in an attempt to thwart Negro emigration. In 1841, after traveling through Philadelphia, an English Quaker, Joseph Sturge, met with former Illinois Governor Edward Coles. Writes Sturge:

> In the course of conversation, the Governor spoke of the prejudice against colour prevailing here as much stronger than in the slave States [the South]. I may add, from my own observation, and much concurring testimony, that Philadelphia appears to be the metropolis of this odious prejudice, and that there is probably no city in the known world, where dislike, amounting to hatred of the coloured population, prevails more than in the city of brotherly love!

Thousands of similar eyewitness accounts could be given.[46]

FACT 32

THE NORTH DOESN'T WANT YOU TO KNOW THAT THE AMERICAN SLAVE TRADE BEGAN IN THE NORTH

Contrary to what we have been taught, America's black slave trade was not born in the South. It was a product of the North. This is why the only slave ships to ever sail from the U.S. left from Northern ports, this is why all were commanded by Northern captains and funded by Northern businessmen, and it is why all of them operated under the auspices of the U.S. flag.

The South, on the other hand, did not own slave ships and never traded in foreign slaves. Her slavery was strictly domestic. This is one of the reasons she banned the foreign slave trade in the Confederacy's new Constitution, penned by the Confederate Founding Fathers in 1861.

The devilish success of The Great Yankee Coverup has obliterated these facts, however. Thus, while no slave ship ever flew under the Confederate Flag, it is this very flag that is today universally viewed as a "symbol of slavery"!

Early Northern politicians were well aware that they could not fool the public about the origins of slavery simply by deflecting the entire issue onto the South. One of these was U.S. Representative Jonathan Ogden Mosely of Connecticut. When, in the late 1700s, the idea of executing slave ship owners by hanging came up before a congressional committee on abolition, the Yankee politician remarked:

> We have been repeatedly told, and told with an air of triumph, by gentlemen from the South, that their citizens have no concern in this infamous traffic; that people from the North are the importers of negroes, and thereby the seducers of Southern citizens to buy them. We have a right to presume, then, that the citizens of the South will entertain no particular partiality for these wicked traffickers, but will be ready to subject them to the most exemplary punishment. So far as the people of Connecticut are concerned, I am sure that, should any citizen of the North be convicted under

this law, so far from thinking it cruel in their Southern brethren to hang them, such a punishment of such culprits would be acknowledged with gratitude as a favor.

Mosely was right! Now we can better understand the words of U.S. Senator Jefferson Davis, soon to become the Southern Confederacy's first and—so far—only president, who, in 1848, rightly chastised his Northern brethren on the Senate floor for their abolitionist hypocrisy:

> You were the men who imported these negroes into this country; you enjoyed the benefits resulting from their carriage and sale; and you reaped the largest profit accruing from the introduction of slaves.[47]

This slave ship, sailing out of New Haven, Connecticut, was just one of thousands that plied the seas in the service of the massive Yankee slave trade, which spanned ports from northern New England and New York City, south to Washington, D.C. and Maryland. There were no Southern slave ports.

FACT 33

THE NORTH DOESN'T WANT YOU TO KNOW THAT AMERICAN SLAVERY GOT ITS START IN THE NORTH

Like the American slave trade (which is connected to but is distinct from American slavery), American slavery also had its beginnings as a legal institution in the North. Its birthplace was, of course, none other than Massachusetts, the very *first* of the original 13 states (colonies) to legalize it in 1641. In contrast, the *last* of the original 13 colonies to legalize slavery was a Southern one, Georgia, which officially sanctioned it 108 years later, in 1749.[48]

Slave auctions like this one in downtown Boston, Massachusetts, were once an everyday scene in countless cities and towns across the Old North.

FACT 34

THE NORTH DOESN'T WANT YOU TO KNOW THAT THE NORTH, NOT THE SOUTH, LAUNCHED BOTH THE AMERICAN SLAVE TRADE & AMERICAN SLAVERY

In 1638 Massachusetts instigated the American slave trade when Boston began importing African slaves commercially for the first time. This occurred when Captain William Pierce brought New England's first remunerative shipload of Africans from the West Indies aboard the 120-ton Salem vessel *Desire*, built at Marblehead, Massachusetts, in 1636.

As mentioned, just three years later, in 1641, Massachusetts gave birth to American slavery when it became the first colony to legitimatize and monetize the institution. By 1676 Boston slavers were routinely coming home with shiploads of human cargo from East Africa and Madagascar. By 1775 Massachusetts had over 5,000 black slaves and 30,000 bondservants.[49]

Contrary to Yankee myth, both the American slave trade and American slavery got their start in the North, in 17th-Century Massachusetts to be exact.

FACT 35

THE NORTH DOESN'T WANT YOU TO KNOW THAT THE AMERICAN ABOLITION MOVEMENT WAS BORN IN THE SOUTH

While Northern colonies like Massachusetts were busy legalizing slavery and expanding the slave trade, Southern colonies—who considered anything connected to human bondage as an "evil"—were busy trying to put a stop to both.

Indeed, America's first voluntary emancipation took place in 1655 in a Southern colony, Virginia, the same state that launched the American abolition movement. This occurred as early as 1753, when Virginia began issuing a series of official statutes in an attempt to block the importation of slaves. In 1732, when English military officer James Edward Oglethorpe founded the Southern colony of Georgia, it became the first to place a prohibition against commercial trafficking in slaves into her state constitution, calling the institution "unjust and cruel." North Carolina and South Carolina both passed restrictions on the trade in 1787, as did Tennessee in 1805.

In point of fact, at one time or another *all* of the antebellum Southern states tried to stop both the importation of slaves and the kidnaping and selling of slaves within their borders. In other words, the reality is that *up until the year 1800, nearly all Southerners were abolitionists.*

As all of this was transpiring, the Northern states were busy bringing in as many African slaves as possible through their seaports. In 1776 alone, for example, the year the Declaration of Independence was issued, New Hampshire imported 627 slaves; Massachusetts imported 3,500; Rhode Island, 4,376; Connecticut, 6,000; New Jersey, 7,600; Delaware, 9,000; New York, 15,000; and Maryland, 80,000.

In 1835, when Yankee tourist Professor Ethan Allen Andrews deceptively told a Virginia slave owner that "the whole public sentiment of the North is decidedly opposed to slavery," the man replied sharply: "So also is that of the South, with but a few exceptions." After visiting the South in the early 1800s, British-American scientist George William Featherstonhaugh wrote:

> All Christian men must unite in the wish that slavery was extinguished in every part of the world, and from my personal knowledge of the sentiments of many of the leading gentlemen in the Southern States, I am persuaded that they look to the ultimate abolition of slavery with satisfaction.

There were a number of good reasons for the near universal abolitionism across Dixie, as Featherstonhaugh commented:

> At the South . . . humanitarianism though of positive weight was but one of several factors. The distinctively Southern considerations against the trade were that its continuance would lower the prices of slaves already on hand, or at least prevent those prices from rising; that it would so increase the staple exports as to spoil the world's market for them; that it would drain out money and keep the community in debt; that it would retard the civilization of the negroes already on hand; and that by raising the proportion of blacks in the population it would intensify the danger of slave insurrections.

Of the 130 American abolition societies established before 1827 by Northern abolitionist Benjamin Lundy, over 100, comprising four-fifths of the total membership, were in the South. Southern Quakers were among the first to protest the spread of the institution. Other Southerners of note who came out against the "peculiar institution" were Bishop William Meade, Christopher Gadsden, Nathaniel Macon, Samuel Doak, Gideon Blackburn, John Rankin, David Nelson, James H. Dickey, James Gilliland, Samuel Crothers, Dyer Burgess, James Lemen, Edward Coles, William T. Allan, James A. Thome, William Ladd, James G. Birney, and George Bourne, cofounder of the "American Anti-Slavery Society" in 1833.

America's most famous early Southern abolitionists included George Washington, Patrick Henry, James Madison, St. George Tucker, and Thomas Jefferson, the latter whose complaints regarding Britain's laws forcing slavery on the original 13 colonies helped lead to the American Revolution.[50]

FACT 36

THE NORTH DOESN'T WANT YOU TO KNOW THAT AMERICA'S FIRST KNOWN LEGAL SLAVE OWNER WAS A BLACK MAN

America's first known official slave owner was Anthony Johnson, an Angolan who came to the colonies as a black African servant. After his arrival in 1621, he worked off his term of indenture and began purchasing human chattel in Virginia, where he accrued great wealth and a large plantation. Later, in the chronicles of Northampton County, there is record of a suit brought by Johnson "for the purpose of recovering his negro servant."

This being the first case of it kind, Johnson, who owned both black and white slaves, helped launch the American slave trade by forcing authorities to legally define the meaning of "slave ownership." In 1652 his son John Johnson imported and bought eleven white slaves, who worked under him at his Virginia plantation, located on the banks of the Pungoteague River.[51]

Anthony Johnson, a black Angolan servant in Virginia, is America's first known official slave owner. With his vast wealth he purchased a spacious plantation, which he ran with the help of both his black and white slaves.

FACT 37

THE NORTH DOESN'T WANT YOU TO KNOW THAT SLAVERY IS NOT A "PECULIAR INSTITUTION" BUT A UNIVERSAL ONE

The uninformed have long referred to American slavery, and more specifically Southern slavery, as the "peculiar institution." Actually, there was nothing "peculiar" about it, and neither was it Southern, for it was once a common worldwide practice.

Slavery is one of the world's oldest institutions, and has been found, in one form or another, on every continent and among every people, society, race, and religion.

Indeed, slavery has been embraced by every known civilization, people, race, society, culture, and religion around the globe, from earliest recorded history right into present-day America. Some of the more notable slaving peoples have been the Egyptians, Assyrians, Babylonians, Sumerians, Akkadians, Mesopotamians, Phoenicians, Mycenaeans, Arameans, East Indians, Chaldeans, Hittites, Scythians, Persians, Arabians, Hebrews, Europeans, and Native-Americans, all who have a long history of enslaving their own citizens and their neighbors.

An institution that has been found among nearly every people and on every continent since prehistoric times can hardly be considered "peculiar." In fact, as this very section shows, it would be more appropriately and accurately called the universal, standard, ordinary, or everyday institution.[52]

FACT 38

THE NORTH DOESN'T WANT YOU TO KNOW THAT WE ALL DESCEND FROM SLAVES & SLAVE OWNERS

No one knows who actually invented slavery of course, for it was a worldwide phenomenon that arose simultaneously around the globe. But we do know that it dates from prehistory, was once universally accepted on every part of the planet, and that at one time it was found on every continent and in every nation. As one historian puts it, "so far as we can trace back the history of the human race, we discover the existence of slavery."

Slavery was, in fact, the economic system upon which *all* ancient civilizations were built, for "slavery is the precursor to civilization." As such it must certainly be counted as one of humanity's oldest social institutions and an essential feature of both society and economics. It is, as the *Encyclopedia Britannica* says, a universal, useful, indispensable, and inevitable accompaniment of human culture, one that eventually became so taken for granted that it was seen as a "divinely ordained institution" in every country.

In 1837, America's seventh vice president, South Carolinian John C. Calhoun, rightly noted that

> there has never yet existed a wealthy and civilized society in which one portion of the community did not, in fact, live on the labor of the other.

This means that slavery is a natural byproduct of human society, placing it alongside our other oldest human social institutions: hunting and gathering, religion, marriage, warfare, puberty rites, funerary rites, and prostitution.[53] Indeed, anthropologists consider slavery not an indication of barbarity, but an early sign of civilization: its emergence meant that humans had begun to enslave rather than kill one another.

From its appearance in the prehistoric mists of time, slavery went on to be employed by the Mesopotamians (ancient Iraqis), Indians, Chinese, ancient Egyptians, Hebrews, Greeks, and Romans. In the pre-Columbian Americas slavery became an integral part of such Native-American peoples as the Maya and Inca, who depended on large scale slave labor in warfare and farming.

The reality is that slavery is a worldwide, omnipresent phenomenon, one that stubbornly persists into modern times, and which dates far back into the fog of the Neolithic Period on all continents, and among all races, ethnic groups, religions, societies, and peoples. All of us then, no matter what our race, color, or nationality, have ancestors who enslaved others and who were themselves enslaved. *We are all descendants of slaves and slave owners.*[54]

Blacks, whites, browns, reds, and yellows have been enslaving their own kind, as well as their neighbors, for thousands of years. For example, my Viking ancestors (pictured here) were ardent slavers who subjugated thousands of fellow whites as they rampaged across Europe in the 8th and 9th Centuries. We all—no matter what our race or nationality—carry the blood of slavery in our veins.

FACT 39

THE NORTH DOESN'T WANT YOU TO KNOW THAT SLAVERY IS A BUSINESS, NOT A RACIST INSTITUTION

Africans, Native-Americans, Europeans, Asians, and Middle-Easterners, all peoples and races, in fact, were enslaving their own kind long before they discovered that there were colors and varieties of humans different than themselves. This can only mean that slavery is a business, one that has nothing to do with race.

Let us take an example, Western slavery, which has its roots among Caucasians. Besides the overwhelming evidence of white-on-white slavery across ancient and Medieval Europe, any doubts about its Caucasoid origins vanish when we examine the etymology of the word slave itself: slave derives from the word "Slav," from the name of a European people, the Slavs, today the largest European ethnic and language group inhabiting central and eastern Europe, as well as Siberia. (All 225 million speak one of the Slavonic languages.)

The word Slav became synonymous with slavery due to the enslavement, by other Europeans (mainly Celts), of thousands of Slavic individuals during Europe's early history. As their names indicate, the Slovenes (of *Slove*nia), the Slovaks (of *Slova*kia), and the Yugoslavians (of Yugo*slavia*), are the modern (white) descendants of the ancient Slavs.

Whites were enthusiastically still enslaving one another right into the 20th Century and beyond. Soviet dictator Joseph Stalin, for example, enslaved some 18 million Caucasians during his reign of terror in the 1930s (thus Stalin owned 14.5 million more *white* slaves than the American South owned *black* slaves), while between 1941 and 1945 nearly 8 million Caucasians were enslaved across Europe under Nazi Germany, including children as young as six years of age (4.5 million more than Dixie).

Under socialist leader Adolf Hitler, white European families were routinely separated and forced to work in factories, fields, and mines, where they were dehumanized, beaten, whipped, and starved by their German overlords. White Nazi slavery was the largest revival of the institution in the 20th Century, and one of the fastest and most monumental expansions of slavery in world history. This appalling event occurred a mere 70 years ago, demolishing the Yankee-New South myth that slavery is a white racist institution.[55]

Slavery has nothing to do with racism and never has. Slavers will enslave anyone they can, no matter what their skin color. Europeans, for example, have been enslaving fellow whites for thousands of years, dating back to early Greece and Rome. The word slave itself derives from *Slav*, the name of a European people. This Caucasian female slave is being sold at auction in London, England.

FACT 40

THE NORTH DOESN'T WANT YOU TO KNOW THAT AFRICA HAS ALWAYS BEEN THE MOST SLAVE DEPENDENT REGION IN THE WORLD

No region on earth has been more dependent on slavery over a longer period of time, practiced slavery more aggressively and widely on its own populace, or allowed slavery to become more entrenched, than Africa. Africa has been so intimately involved with slavery over such an immense duration—with slave majorities thought to be as high as 90 percent of the population in some regions—that its name is today synonymous with the institution. "The great womb of slavery," Yankee abolitionist Charles Sumner correctly called it.

Slavery was so intrinsic to the early African way of life that at one time slaves, known by their own people as "black ivory," could be found in nearly every African society, where—as in every other country where slavery is found—the minority population dominated and enslaved the majority population. These were not merely "insignificant traces of slavery," as African apologists maintain, but rather true African slave societies, built on and around the bondage of their own people, employing some of the most brutal and sadistic forms of slavery ever recorded.

Slavery's pivotal role in African society certainly explains why not a single organized slave revolt, or even an abolition movement for that matter, ever arose among the African populace during the entire pre-colonial period, and it is why slavery was finally only outlawed by the efforts of non-Africans (mainly Europeans).

It also explains why there has long been a belief among the native population that due to domestic African slavery, "the whole land has been laid under a curse which will never be removed."[56]

FACT 41

THE NORTH DOESN'T WANT YOU TO KNOW THAT AFRICAN SLAVERY BEGAN IN AFRICA, NOT AMERICA

Africans were practicing slavery on themselves for thousands of years before the arrival of Europeans. In point of fact, "African slavery was coeval with the existence of the African race . . . . [and thus] has existed in Africa since its first [negro] settlement," predating even the founding of ancient Egypt over 5,000 years ago.

It cannot be stressed enough that, it being a "characteristic part of African tradition" and a truly "universal" aspect of African society, *African slavery was of African origin.* Thus indigenous African slavery is nearly as old as Africa itself. Indeed, not only were slaves an integral part of the commerce of prehistoric and ancient Africa, but just as in early Sudan, as only one example, slave ownership was an accepted sign of wealth, and so was considered no different than owning precious metals or gems. Even the practice of exporting African slaves out of the country can be definitively dated back to at least the 5th Century B.C. It can be truly said then that *early Africa literally revolved around the enslavement of its own people by its own rulers upon its own soil.*

The native victims of the pre-conquest African slave trade were captured inland or in East Africa by their African brethren, then exported to Persia, Arabia, India, and China. This means that the first European slavers to venture to Africa (Portuguese ship captain Antonio Gonzales arrived in 1434 and purchased several native African boys who he sold in Spain, while Portugal's trade in slaves with the continent began in 1441) only interrupted the booming, "well-developed" slave trade inaugurated by West Africans and various coastal tribes—one that had already been going on there for untold centuries with peoples like the Arabs. It was only much later that Europeans helped stimulate the existing domestic business.[57]

FACT 42

THE NORTH DOESN'T WANT YOU TO KNOW THAT AFRICA ENGAGED IN THE TRANSATLANTIC SLAVE TRADE FOR ITS ENTIRE 424 YEARS

Pre-European Africa had been practicing slavery, servitude, vassalage, and serfdom on its own people for thousands of years (in forms far more brutal than anything found in the American South), dating back to before the continent's Iron Age, to the very dawn of African history itself. In fact, Africa is the *only* region that engaged *continually* in the West African-European-American slave trade for its full 424 years, from start to finish.

It was just such facts that made the institution so understandable to many American black civil rights leaders. One of these was African-American educator, intellectual, and author William E. B. Du Bois, who wrote that he could forgive slavery for it "is a world-old habit."⁵⁸

This old illustration depicts a typical African slave raid, this particular one occurring in Digby in the 1800s. According to one at the scene of the attack, a tribe viciously assaulted its neighbors in the dead of night, capturing and carrying off hundreds of individuals. As described by the eyewitness, those who resisted were mercilessly tortured and killed. Note the dismemberments and beheadings, as well as the baby being tossed into the air and impaled on a spear. Such slave raids were once the norm in Africa, and in fact, continue in parts of the continent to this day.

FACT 43

THE NORTH DOESN'T WANT YOU TO KNOW THAT AFRICA IS RESPONSIBLE FOR ENSLAVING & SELLING HER OWN PEOPLE

What Yankee historians, New South professors, and the Liberal media will not tell you is that Africans were never actually hunted down and captured directly by the white crews of foreign slave ships. They were captives who had already been taken during yearly intertribal raids and then enslaved by enterprising African kings, kinglets, chiefs, and subchiefs, who quite eagerly traded them to non-African slavers for rum, guns, gunpowder, textiles, beads, iron, and cloth.

Sometimes these intra-African militaristic style raids and battles were carried on by slave armies led by slave officers. Though the attrition rate was extremely high (over the millennia millions upon millions of Africans died during these marauding attacks), greedy African kings would often purposefully start such wars, known as "slave hunts," in order to obtain slaves, a practice that eventually became "endemic" across large swaths of the continent.

In other words, it was African chiefs who first enslaved other Africans, and it was African slave merchants—slave drivers known as *slattees*—who then forcibly marched them to the coast in chains and sold them to Arabs, Europeans, and eventually Yankees. This means that when it came to African slaves, *all* of the slave hunting, slave capturing, slave abusing, slave torturing, slave marching, slave marketing, slave dealing, and slave selling went on *inside* Africa, perpetuated by Africans on other Africans on African land.

This is why before 1820 no free blacks ever came to the U.S. from Africa. All were imported as slaves—that is, they had already been in bondage in their native country.

To put it another way, during the transatlantic slave trade, every one of the Africans brought to America on Yankee slave ships had already been enslaved in their home country by fellow Africans, after which they were marched to the Slave Coast (a 240-mile maritime strip roughly extending between the Volta River and the Akinga River), temporarily held in stockades (prisons), then sold to white slavers by local African governments.

In short, whites only "bought slaves after they had been captured," and thus played no role in the actual enslaving process that took place in the interior, and had no idea what went on beyond the coastal areas. As one Yankee slave ship owner put it in the late 1700s:

> It is true, I have brought these slaves from Africa; but I have only transported them from one master to another.

Yes, *African slavery was purely an African-on-African business.*

And here is proof: until the first part of the 19th Century, no white man had ever set foot in the interior of tropical Africa. Even the Europeans who first came to Africa's shores in the 1400s had no knowledge of anything "south of the desert." These were the African hinterlands, after all: utterly unnavigable and therefore unexplorable, due not just to the ferocity of the native animals, but because it swarmed with cannibalistic tribes who practiced human sacrifice and other primitive customs.

At one time even radical abolitionists admitted as much. In 1835 Reverend George Bourne—the Briton who inspired fanatical New England abolitionist William Lloyd Garrison—noted that "no ancient and accessible part of the inhabited globe is so completely unknown as the interior of Africa." Thus whites could not have had any knowledge of what went on in the central regions of the continent during most of the Atlantic slave trade.

Truly, without Africa's encouragement, commitment, participation, and collusion there would have been no black slavery in America. It is obvious then that Africa herself must be held accountable for taking part in the enslavement and forced deportation of some 10 to 50 million of her own people during the four hundred years between the 15th and the 19th Centuries.[59]

FACT 44

THE NORTH DOESN'T WANT YOU TO KNOW THAT WHITE SLAVERY WAS ONCE A WORLDWIDE PHENOMENA

Our leftist schools focus only on black slavery, completely ignoring the reality of white slavery—and for good reason: America's liberalistic teachers do not want the truth to be known, for it would expose and demolish their false teachings about white racism and capitalism. Here we will correct this imbalance.

Not only did American slavery exist among native peoples—for example, the Aztecs, Incas, and Mayans—long before the arrival of Christopher Columbus (the man responsible for starting the European-American slave trade), but Western slavery itself began as a purely white man's occupation, one that had nothing to do with Indians, Africans, or any other people of color, or even racism.

Indeed, historically speaking, *both the earliest known slave traders and the earliest known slaves were Caucasians*, as we have noted: the Babylonians, Assyrians, Sumerians, Akkadians, Mesopotamians, Phoenicians, Egyptians, Mycenaeans, Arameans, East Indians, Chaldeans, Hittites, Scythians, Persians, Arabians, and Hebrews—at some point in their history—all either enslaved other whites or were themselves enslaved by other whites. In India, for example, historic records show that Caucasian slavery was being practiced by 1750 B.C., nearly 4,000 years ago, though doubtlessly it arose there thousands of years earlier. Some maintain that white thralldom may have even once been an integral part of Hinduism, one of the world's oldest religions.

The Vikings, Celts, Greeks, Italians, British, French, and, in fact, all European peoples, once enslaved other whites, a practice that has endured into the present day. As discussed, in the 1940s Hitler enslaved nearly 8 million Caucasians, while in the 1930s Stalin enslaved as many as 18 million whites.[60]

FACT 45

THE NORTH DOESN'T WANT YOU TO KNOW THAT AFRICA ONCE POSSESSED 1.5 MILLION WHITE SLAVES

At one time there were so many white slaves in Africa that a series of wars, known as the Barbary Wars, were fought and an abolition society, known as the "Knights Liberators of the White Slaves in Africa," was formed to rescue and emancipate them.

One of the many sea battles that took place during the Barbary Wars, a massive Euro-American effort to free Africa's white slaves.

The primary period of the enslavement of whites by African peoples lasted some 300 years, roughly from the 16th Century to the 19th Century. It has been conservatively estimated that between the years 1500 and 1800, 1 million to 1.5 million whites—from both Europe and America—were enslaved by the Barbary States, with an average of 5,000 white slaves entering the region each year. At about 14 new whites being imported a day, it was a commonplace occurrence. The city of Algiers, the capital of the African nation of Algeria, alone possessed some 25,000 to 50,000 European bondsmen and women. Over the centuries countless tens of thousands of additional whites were killed during the process of enslavement.

The Barbary Wars were comprised of several full scale U.S. military campaigns, launched in an effort to put a stop to the merciless enslavement of white Christians in Africa: the Tripolitan War (or First Barbary War, 1801-1805) under President Thomas Jefferson, and the Algerian War (or Second Barbary War, 1815) under President James Madison. Shortly thereafter, in 1816, the British, led by Lord Exmouth (Edward Pellew), conducted their own assault on African white slavery in the famed conflict known as the "Battle of Algiers."[61]

FACT 46

THE NORTH DOESN'T WANT YOU TO KNOW THAT AFRICAN SLAVE OWNERS TREATED THEIR WHITE & BLACK SLAVES FAR WORSE THAN ANYTHING KNOWN IN AMERICA

Surviving records reveal that Africa's black slave owners treated both their black and white slaves with absolute savagery, daily subjecting them to appalling forms of abuse and even torture that included whipping, branding, starvation, exposure, and beheading. One example of how they handled their personal African slaves will suffice:

> On the death of a king, or a distinguished [African] chief, hundreds of their courtiers, wives, and slaves are put to death, in order that they may have the benefit of their attendance in the future world. It often happens, that where the sword of the rude warrior is once drawn in such cases, it is not again readily sheathed; whole towns may be depopulated before the thirst for blood is satiated.

African kings were a brutal lot who once regularly enslaved their neighbors, and later Europeans.

Thus in 1800 the funeral of Ashanti King Quamina was accompanied by the ritual murder of 200 African slaves. On another occasion the Ashanti people slaughtered some 2,600 African slaves at a single public sacrifice. In 1873, when the British seized Kumasi, a city in southern central Ghana, they discovered a huge brass bowl five feet in diameter. In it the Ashanti had collected the blood of countless thousands of sacrificed African slaves and used it to wash the footstools of deceased African kings.

Once, when the mother of a certain Ashanti king died, 3,000 African slaves were sacrificed at her tomb, and for two months afterward 200 additional slaves were put to death every week "in her honor." Did anything in the American South ever compare to such horrific savagery?[62]

FACT 47

THE NORTH DOESN'T WANT YOU TO KNOW THAT WHITE AMERICAN SLAVERY LAID THE GROUNDWORK FOR BLACK AMERICAN SLAVERY

The vast majority of white immigrants who came to America's original 13 English colonies—at least two-thirds—came as white servants. Made up primarily of English, Germans, Irish, and Scots, some 400,000 whites formed the first non American servant population in the region's history, working as unskilled laborers on the budding nation's large new plantations.

For millennia white slavery was standard practice throughout Europe, after which it spread to the Americas, where it laid the foundation for African slavery.

White indentured servitude, being much preferred over African slavery (Africans were considered "alien" by early white colonialists), *was the institution that paved the way for black slavery in America*; or as the late 19th-Century New England historian Jeffrey R. Brackett put it, white slavery made "a smoother pathway for the growth of [black] slavery."

In 1698, as just one example, not only were there more white servants in Virginia than there were Africans, but white indentured servants were being imported in far greater numbers than blacks at the time.[63]

FACT 48

THE NORTH DOESN'T WANT YOU TO KNOW THAT NEW YORK WAS FOUNDED TO SERVE AS A SLAVE STATE & NEW YORK CITY WAS FOUNDED TO SERVE AS A SLAVE PORT

Originally known as New Amsterdam, New York City grew to become the center of the Dutch colony of what was then called New Netherland (later renamed New York by the English), a territory founded in 1624 and governed by the great slave trading corporation, the Dutch West India Company, whose primary goal was to "extend the market for its human merchandise whithersoever its influence reached." Today New York City's official flag still bears the colors of the original flag flown by Netherland's slave ships: blue, orange, and white.

Thus it was that slavery took root in New York at the very beginning, when it was established by the Dutch in 1624. This marked the start of the official recognition of slavery in the middle colonies, where the institution quickly became a "custom" in the region.

Both New York and New York City were developed around slavery, the former as a slave trading center, the latter as a slave port.

The location of New York state, and more importantly, New York City, was not accidental. The Dutch had carefully and intentionally chosen them, not only for their many protected inlets, but also for their strategic positions, situated midway between the Northern and Southern colonies. From here they hoped to maximize slave sales and further spread their slave trading business throughout the Eastern seaboard.[64]

FACT 49

THE NORTH DOESN'T WANT YOU TO KNOW THAT NEW YORK CITY WAS AMERICA'S SLAVING CAPITAL FOR OVER A CENTURY

By the time the slavery-obsessed English took over the colony of New Netherland in 1664 and renamed it New York, it "contained more slaves in proportion to its inhabitants than Virginia." From then on the institution only increased. Between 1697 and 1790, for example, Albany's slave population grew from 3 percent to 16 percent. Influential Albany plantation owners, like the Schuyler and Van Rensselaer families, made vast fortunes using black slaves to build up their estates. A number of their well-known homes stand in New York's capital city to this day, including Ten Broeck Manor, Cherry Hill Mansion, and the Schuyler Mansion.

In 1665 New York passed Duke's Laws, named after the Duke of York (who later became King James II). A codification of statutes borrowed from the Massachusetts Fundamentals (a set of early colonial laws), they allowed Indians and blacks who had not been baptized into the Christian religion to be enslaved.

By the year 1700 New York Harbor was teeming with slave ships and slavery had become the foundation of the state's economy. New Yorkers believed that their "peculiar institution" was so vital to Northern finance that they blocked and delayed emancipation for over 100 years, with so-called "official abolition" not occurring until 1827. New York's slave owners were a brutal lot, engaging in a myriad of cruel practices, from disenfranchisement and the separation of slave families to whipping, torture, and murder.

By the year 1720 New York had become one of the largest slaveholding states in the North, with 4,000 slaves against a white population of only 31,000. The situation was unbearable to the North's few abolitionists, resulting in the nation's first antislavery essay: *The Selling of Joseph*, penned in Massachusetts by the famed Yankee judge who presided at the Salem witch trials, Samuel Sewall. As in ancient Africa, Israel, and Thrace, slaves were such a valuable commodity in the American North that they could be used as an insurance policy to cover their master's financial obligations, or be sold to pay off the owner's creditors. This led to the illegal Northern practice of falsely claiming free blacks as "personal property," then selling them to pay off debts.

By the mid 1700s one-sixth of New York City's population was comprised of African slaves. By 1756 New York state possessed some 13,000 adult black slaves, giving it the dubious distinction of having the largest slave force of any Northern colony at the time. That same year slaves accounted for 25 percent of the population in Kings, Queens, Richmond, New York City, and Westchester, making these areas the primary bastion of American slavery throughout the rest of the colonial period.

New Englanders moving south to Westchester and Long Island were among the most eager slave purchasers, and by 1750 at least one-tenth of the province of New York's householders were slave owners. At New York City's peak, at least one-fifth of the town's population were slaves. Little wonder that in 1785 New York's state legislators rejected a bill advocating gradual emancipation. In 1860 alone it has been estimated that 85 vessels—all which had been fitted out in and which had sailed from New York City—brought as many as 60,000 African slaves into the U.S.

What Northern and New South historians will not tell you is that there is only one reason that New York City is today America's largest and wealthiest municipality: for centuries it served as the literal heart of North America's slaving industry. Some of the most famous New York names, in fact—names such as the Lehman Brothers, John Jacob Astor, Junius and Pierpont Morgan, Charles Tiffany, Archibald Gracie, and many others—are only known today because of the tremendous riches their families made from the town's highly profitable slave business.

Many of the 21st-Century's wealthiest New York Jewish families descend from 18th-Century Jewish slave ship owners and slave traders, who eagerly participated with Northern colonial Christians in the Yankee's "peculiar institution." You will never learn any of this from pro-North mainstream history books, for their anti-South authors and publishers have a deeply vested interest in hiding the truth.[65]

FACT 50

THE NORTH DOESN'T WANT YOU TO KNOW THAT NEW YORK PRACTICED SLAVERY LONGER THAN ANY OTHER STATE

New York City, the center of America's cotton business as early as 1815, was so deeply connected to the Yankee slave trade and to Southern slavery that it opposed all early attempts at abolition within its borders, and, along with New Jersey, was the last Northern state to resist the passage of emancipation laws.

Being America's slave state capital, it is not surprising that New York practiced slavery for an astonishing 239 years:

1. Slavery in New York officially began (on the island of Manhattan) under the Dutch, and lasted for 38 years, from 1626 to 1664.

2. New York slavery then fell under the auspices of the English, lasting for 112 years, from 1664 to 1776.

3. After the formation of the U.S., New York slavery was turned over to the new state government, continuing on for another 51 years, from 1776 to 1827, when it was legally "abolished."

4. Slavery in New York then persisted illegally for another 38 years, only being permanently shut down by the ratification of the Thirteenth Amendment in December 1865.

New York's 239-year history of slavery is the longest of any state, and certainly far longer than any Southern state. It is greater even than Massachusetts, where both the American slave trade and American slavery got their start. This makes New York America's premier slave state, our one and only true slavocracy, prompting one early historian to refer to the Empire State as a slave "regime never paralleled in equal volume elsewhere."[66]

114 ∾ THE GREAT YANKEE COVERUP

FACT 51

THE NORTH DOESN'T WANT YOU TO KNOW THAT IN 1776 THE NORTHERN STATES HAD MORE SLAVES THAN THE SOUTH

In 1776, at the time of the formation of the *first* Confederate States of America, the USA, of the 500,000 slaves in the 13 colonies, 300,000 (or 60 percent) were possessed by the Northern ones, only 200,000 (or 40 percent) by the Southern ones. It was only later, when Yankee slave traders actively pushed slavery even further south, that Dixie came to possess more slaves than the North.[67]

Two black female slaves serve a white family in Concord, Massachusetts, where freed slaves were later segregated and forced to live in shacks around Walden Pond. As the birthplace of both American slavery and the American slave trade, it is only natural that slaves were once an integral aspect of Northern white society. Indeed, up until the late 1700s, the North possessed far more slaves than the South. It was only when the racist Yankee found slavery unprofitable and the presence of blacks intolerable that he began pushing his slaves on the Southern states. Not in an effort to abolish it in the North, but to foster it in the South, where Yankee businessmen hoped to continue to reap huge profits from selling slaves and buying slave-produced products like cotton.

FACT 52

THE NORTH DOESN'T WANT YOU TO KNOW THAT THE PERCENTAGE OF YANKEE SLAVE OWNERS WAS ALWAYS HIGHER THAN SOUTHERN ONES

By 1690, in Perth Amboy, New Jersey, as just one example of the Northern colonies, nearly every white inhabitant owned one or more black slaves, and by 1775, 12 percent of the population of eastern New Jersey was comprised of slaves. This means that almost 100 percent of the whites in some Northern cities were slaveholders.

Other Northern states shared similar statistics from this time period. Records from the early 1700s reveal that 42 percent of all New York households owned slaves, and that the share of slaves in both New York and New Jersey was larger than that of North Carolina.

Percentage wise slave ownership was always much higher in the Old North than in the Old South. Here, in Providence, Rhode Island, a white slave owner is selling one of his slaves to a plantation owner in New Jersey, necessitating breaking up the slave family.

Contrast all of this with the Old South, where at no time did white slave owners make up more than 4.8 percent of the total population (only 25 percent of Southern households possessed one or more slaves), the peak number in 1860. And as one moves further back in time these figures sharply decrease. In fact, in most Southern towns there were no slave owners.

The conclusion? The percentage of slaveholders in the Old North was always much higher than slaveholders in the Old South. Do not be fooled by anti-South writers who tell you otherwise.[68]

FACT 53

THE NORTH DOESN'T WANT YOU TO KNOW THAT YANKEES REGISTERED THEIR SLAVES AS "LIVESTOCK," SOUTHERNERS AS FAMILY MEMBERS

From early American records it is quite apparent that Northerners had far less regard for their African-American slaves than Southerners. For instance, the Massachusetts general court evaluated both red and black slaves as "private property" suitable for exportation as "merchandise," while Rhode Island and New Hampshire more specifically taxed them as "livestock."

Northern slave owners called their human chattel "slaves" and viewed them as livestock. Southern slave owners referred to their human chattel as "servants" and saw them as part of their family.

New Jersey and Pennsylvania—the latter state where blacks were present even before slave owner William Penn's colony was founded—preferred to see their slaves as assessable possessions, while New York evaluated its slaves using a poll tax. Everywhere across the North, in fact, black slaves were registered by Yankee families on the same lists as their horses, cattle, tools, kitchen goods, and other common farm and household items.

How different from the South, where slaves were civilly registered as literal members of the families of their white, black, red, or brown owners, and, in nearly all cases, stringently cared for throughout their entire lives, very much as if they were the adopted children of their masters. Little wonder that many Southern blacks did not welcome emancipation, preferring servitude instead.[69]

FACT 54

THE NORTH DOESN'T WANT YOU TO KNOW THAT THERE WERE FEW LAWS PROTECTING SLAVES IN THE NORTHERN STATES

Yankee slave owners had complete freedom to discipline their chattel in any manner they saw fit, and various barbarities—from whipping and branding, to public torture and burning slaves at the stake—were legal, routine, and socially accepted.

A popular pastime in the Old North was the slave execution, a public spectacle attended by entire families. This New York slave is being burned at the stake for a minor infraction of the state's strict Black Codes.

In New York, for instance, where a 1702 law authorized masters to chastise their human property "at their own discretion," slaves convicted of heinous crimes, such as murder, were subject to all manner of hideous fates. These included being "burned at the stake," "gibbeted alive," and "broken on the wheel."

This is precisely what occurred in 1712, when New York authorities hanged 13 slaves, burned four of them alive (one over a "slow fire"), "broke" one on the wheel, and left another to starve to death chained to the floor. In 1741 alone the Empire State executed 31 blacks: 13 were burned at the stake, 18 were hanged, while another 71 were transported out of state.

On another occasion a New York slave named Tom, found guilty of killing two people, was ordered to be "roasted over a slow fire so that he will suffer in torment for at least eight to ten hours." Such executions were performed in public, in full view of ordinary New Yorkers.[70]

FACT 55

THE NORTH DOESN'T WANT YOU TO KNOW THAT THERE WERE NUMEROUS LAWS PROTECTING SLAVES IN THE SOUTHERN STATES

In the Old South black servants were protected by a literal bible of hundreds of rigorous rules and regulations, crimes against slaves were punishable by law, and cruel slaveholders, though rare, were harshly penalized (even executed) when caught. The result was that the vast majority of Southern slaves lived lives of comfort, safety, health, and security from birth to death—which is why so many of them, when given a choice, preferred servitude to emancipation.

In 1900 Dr. Henry A. White, history professor at Washington and Lee University, made the following astute comments; words that should be permanently enshrined in granite in the capitol building of every Southern state:

> The [Southern slavery] system produced no paupers and no orphans; food and clothing the negro did not lack; careful attention he received in sickness, and, without a burden [care] the aged servants spent their closing days. The plantation was an industrial school where the negro gradually acquired skill in the use of tools. A bond of affection was woven between Southern masters and servants which proved strong enough in 1861-'65 to keep the negroes at voluntary labour to furnish food for the armies that contended against [Lincoln's] military emancipation.[71] In the planter's home the African learned to set a higher value upon the domestic virtues which he saw illustrated in the lives of Christian men and women; for, be it remembered, the great body of the slave-holders of the South were devotees of the religious faith handed down through pious ancestors from [John] Knox, [Thomas] Cranmer, [John] Wesley, and [John] Bunyan. With truth, perhaps, it may be said than no other economic system before or since that time has engendered a bond of personal affection between capital and labour so strong as that established by the institution of slavery.[72]

FACT 56

THE NORTH DOESN'T WANT YOU TO KNOW THAT WHEN GIVEN A CHOICE BLACK AMERICAN SLAVES PREFERRED TO BE OWNED BY SOUTHERN SLAVEHOLDERS OVER NORTHERN ONES

Unlike in the North, in the South slaves were paid a weekly salary and were given Sundays, rainy days, and holidays off. Southern servants were also permitted time to hunt, fish, and visit loved ones on neighboring farms and plantations. On Saturdays, the day traditionally set aside for Southern servants to work their own land, they labored either a half day, or had the entire day free. Each year they also had several week's worth of work free holidays (such as Christmas, Good Friday, Independence Day, and the post harvest period), with odd days off as rewards.

Southern slaves enjoyed numerous rights, protections, and freedoms, including holidays, sick leave, salaries, and lifelong free healthcare, clothing, food, and shelter. Is it any wonder that these Tennessee slaves are happy?

On many plantations there was a servant-only party held every Saturday night, complete with whiskey, a barbeque, music (items often contributed by the white owners), and dancing. Southern slaves worked from sunrise to early afternoon (eight hours) five days a week, with one to three hours off for lunch. Thus their average work week was 25 to 40 hours long, far below the 75 hour work week of free whites and blacks at the time.

The life of the Southern slave was indeed easy and secure compared to the far more difficult life of the Yankee slave. This is why, when asked, nearly 100 percent of American blacks said they would rather be owned by a Southern slaveholder than a Northern one.[73]

FACT 57

THE NORTH DOESN'T WANT YOU TO KNOW THAT ANTILITERACY SLAVE LAWS WERE A CREATION OF THE LIBERAL NORTH NOT THE CONSERVATIVE SOUTH

Antiliteracy laws, meant to prevent both black slaves and free blacks from learning to read and write, were first invented in the puritanical North, where they were strictly and sometimes violently enforced. As hard evidence for the widespread existence of antiliteracy sentiment, not to mention overt white racism, in the North prior to Lincoln's War, we need look no further than the doleful story of Prudence Crandall.

Prudence Crandall's "School for Colored Girls" being attacked and torched by local townspeople in Canterbury, Connecticut. "Your nigger school shall never be allowed in Canterbury nor in any other town in this State!" the furious Yankee mob shouted. The building was later ripped from its foundation by a team of 100 oxen and destroyed. Crandall was only one of hundreds of Yankee abolitionists who were criticized, harassed, assaulted, and driven from the region for promoting racial equality. Her story highlights the utter disdain the majority of Northerners had for both blacks and abolition at the time.

Crandall was a white New England teacher who founded the "High School for Young Colored Ladies and Misses" in Canterbury,

Connecticut, in 1834. One would think that fellow Yanks, had they—as we have been taught—been true non-racist egalitarians, would have applauded her efforts. Instead, for trying to offer blacks a free education in New England, Crandall, a Quaker and abolitionist, was harassed, persecuted, arrested (three times), imprisoned, and had her home burned down, while Northern white mobs attacked and stoned her school, tore it from its foundations using a team of 100 oxen, then physically drove her out of the state.

None of Connecticut's white population shed a tear for Crandall. Instead, the state, and in particular her politicians, were quite happy to see her, and her school, disappear. Their parting comment perfectly sums up the North's feelings about blacks and black education during this period: "Once open this door, and New-England will become the Liberia of America," they shrieked as Crandall left Connecticut for the final time. New Hampshire whites followed suit by destroying their state's own all-black schools.[74]

The headmaster of a public school in New Hampshire blocks the entrance of a black mother trying to bring her two children to class. After launching American slavery, Yankees discovered that they did not particularly like the idea of living in the midst of blacks, as either slaves or as freemen. Thus began a region-wide campaign to prevent African-Americans from entering mainstream white society, and even deport them en masse from the country. One result was the creation of the American Colonization Society in 1816, whose stated mission was to make America "white from coast to coast." The ACS found its greatest patronage in Yankee cities such as Boston, Massachusetts, where men like Harvard University President Jared Sparks gave it their full backing. But the racist organization found massive support in the white Midwest as well. Abraham Lincoln, for instance, was not only a member, but an Illinois chapter leader as well.

FACT 58

THE NORTH DOESN'T WANT YOU TO KNOW THAT JIM CROW LAWS WERE "UNIVERSAL" IN ALL OF THE NORTHERN STATES, BUT RARE & "UNUSUAL" IN THE OLD SOUTH

Wherever the various races have the least amount of contact, racism tends to increase—no matter what the skin color of the dominant or majority race.

And this is precisely the situation we find in the Old South and the Old North, for in the latter region most whites had little if any interaction with blacks, making racism far more ingrained. Thus we find that Jim Crow laws, along with both legal and customary segregation, for instance, were "universal" in all of the Northern states, but were "unusual" in the South.[75]

Anti-black sentiment was so strong in the Old North that it was actually life-threatening to be antislavery at the time, which is why Yankee abolitionists like Elijah P. Lovejoy of Maine, were never cordially received by fellow Northerners. As is pictured here, Northern anti-abolition mobs repeatedly broke into his publishing office and destroyed his printing equipment. On November 7, 1837, he was cornered in a warehouse in Alton, Illinois, which mobs attempted to set ablaze. When Lovejoy came out to try and prevent torches from being applied to the wooden roof, he was shot to death. He was 34 years old.

FACT 59

THE NORTH DOESN'T WANT YOU TO KNOW THAT YANKEES IMPOSED LIFELONG SLAVERY ON THEIR SLAVES, WHILE IN THE SOUTH SLAVES COULD PURCHASE THEIR FREEDOM ANYTIME

From the beginning of Yankee slavery, African chattel were made slaves for life across the North. In 1663, for example, Maryland passed a slavery law whose first section ordered that

> "all negroes and other slaves within this province, and all negroes and other slaves to be hereafter imported into this province, shall serve during life; and all children born of any negro or other slave, shall be slaves, as their fathers were, for the term of their lives." The second section recites that "divers free-born [white] English women, forgetful of their free condition, and to the disgrace of our nation, do intermarry with negro slaves"; and for deterring from such "shameful matches," it enacts that, during their husbands' lives, white women so intermarrying shall be servants to the masters of their husbands, and that the issue of such marriages shall be slaves for life.

Even when Northern slaves were able to buy their freedom, Yankees thought nothing of recapturing them and reselling them back into slavery, as was the case with this New York freedman in 1836.

It was only much later that this mandate was vetoed in the North, and slaves were allowed to buy their liberty.

In the South, however, from slavery's very inception slaves could purchase their freedom whenever they wished, and thousands did just that. This is yet just one more proof that authentic slavery never existed in Dixie, for lifelong indenture is an element of true thralldom, and this is something that existed only in the North: the birthplace of, and the only home of, genuine American slavery.[76]

FACT 60

THE NORTH DOESN'T WANT YOU TO KNOW THAT SEGREGATION WAS THE NORM IN THE OLD NORTH, BUT WAS COMPLETELY UNKNOWN IN THE ANTEBELLUM SOUTH

Since Jim Crow laws in the South were scarce (and seldom enforced where they existed), it is not surprising that racial segregation was also rare. In fact, during the antebellum period there is not a single known case of segregation anywhere in Dixie. Conversely, it was endemic to America's northeastern states right up to, and far beyond, the 1860s.

The North's onerous Black Codes forbade, among many other things, black immigration and black civil rights, and even banned blacks from attending public schools. Little wonder that those blacks who managed to survive in the North were generally less educated and less skilled than Southern blacks. Up to 1855 it was this very type of oppression that prevented blacks from serving as jurors in all but one Northern state: Massachusetts.

Northern blacks who ignored the region's rigorous segregation laws were severely punished.

Even after Lincoln's fake and illegal Final Emancipation Proclamation was issued (on January 1, 1863), literally nothing changed for African-Americans living north of the Mason-Dixon Line. When former slaves managed to make economic progress there, they found themselves blocked at every turn by a hostile racist Northern government, the very body that had "emancipated" them.

As mentioned, this blockage was accomplished not only by Black Codes, by also through the implementation of extreme Jim Crow laws and public segregation laws, both which were unconditionally and widely supported by the Yankee populace.[77]

FACT 61

THE NORTH DOESN'T WANT YOU TO KNOW THAT NEW YORK WAS ONE OF THE MOST RACIST OF THE NORTHERN STATES

Naturally, New York City, America's slavery capital for decades, had its own set of strict Black Codes, all which were considered particularly savage by humanitarians and abolitionists. Offences by black servants could garner punishments ranging from beatings and whippings to expatriation and even execution. In 1741 the mere hint of a slave revolt resulted in the public killing of 27 Northern slaves, all who were either hanged or burned at the stake.

White New Yorkers as a whole were arguably the most racially intolerant of any of the Northern states, perhaps second only to the citizens of Illinois and Massachusetts. This is certainly why, for instance, New York City had far less black artisans than Southern towns, such as the far more racially tolerant New Orleans.

Between 1702 and 1741 alone the Empire State passed a massive series of statutes that, among other things, allowed blacks convicted of heinous acts to be executed "in such a manner as the enormity of their crimes might be deemed to merit." Along with this law manumissions were restricted, free New York blacks were prohibited from holding real estate, and the state's entire set of Black Codes was strengthened in an effort to gain greater control over both slaves and blacks in general. Well into the 1830s not even free blacks were allowed to drive their own hacks or carts. This same law was also active in Baltimore, Maryland, while in Philadelphia, Pennsylvania, free blacks were not allowed to drive an omnibus.

Hundreds of such illustrations from the racist Old North could be given. No wonder so many blacks wanted to get as far away from Yankeedom as they could, requesting that they be sent as far South as possible (to places like New Orleans), or even out of the country.[78]

FACT 62

THE NORTH DOESN'T WANT YOU TO KNOW THAT AUTHENTIC SLAVERY WAS PRACTICED IN THE NORTH, AUTHENTIC SERVITUDE WAS PRACTICED IN THE SOUTH

Two of the key indicators of *authentic* slavery are that 1) a slave has no rights of any kind, and 2) he or she cannot purchase their freedom. Both of these rights, however, are available under a much milder form of bondage known as servitude, making it completely different than true slavery.

In the North, where black bondsmen were called "slaves," one was more likely to find them working in chains and shackles under the thumb of a racist owner, as can be seen in this early illustration of a New England plantation.

Contrary to the myths of Northern anti-South propagandists, from slavery's first appearance in the South, black servants were accorded a myriad of civil and personal rights, and also could purchase their freedom at any time. In fact, the first blacks in the American South came to this country not as slaves, but as indentured servants, just as most white colonists did at the time.

The truth is that it was in the colonial North, where there were few laws protecting blacks and where slaves could not buy their liberty, that genuine slavery was practiced. What North and New South writers conveniently and slanderously call Southern "slavery" then was actually, as Edward A. Pollard rightly asserts, a "well-guarded and moderate system of negro servitude." As he wrote during Lincoln's War:

In referring to the condition of the negro in this war, we use the term "slavery"... under strong protest. For there is no such thing in the South; it is a term fastened upon us by the exaggeration and conceit of Northern literature, and most improperly acquiesced in by Southern writers. There is a system of African servitude in the South; in which the negro, so far from being under the absolute dominion of his master (which is the true meaning of the vile word "slavery"), has, by law of the land, his personal rights recognized and protected, and his comfort and "right" of "happiness" consulted, and by the practice of the system, has a sum of individual indulgences, which makes him altogether the most striking type in the world of cheerfulness and contentment. And the system of servitude in the South has this peculiarity over other systems of servitude in the world: that it does not debase one of God's creatures from the condition of free-citizenship and membership in organized society and [which] thus rest on acts of debasement and disenfranchisement, but [instead it] elevates a savage, and rests on the solid basis of human improvement. The European mind, adopting the nomenclature of our enemies, has designated as "slavery" what is really the most virtuous system of servitude in the world.[79]

In the South, where black bondsmen were referred to as "servants," one was more likely to find them working in informal conditions, without supervision under the auspices of a tolerant easygoing owner. Note the relaxed strolling "slaves" in this early drawing of a typical Southern tobacco plantation, a Victorian illustration that I used for the cover of my book, *Slavery 101*.

FACT 63

THE NORTH DOESN'T WANT YOU TO KNOW THAT THE NORTHERN STATES NEVER ACTUALLY OFFICIALLY ABOLISHED SLAVERY

Anti-South writers tell us that the Northern states "abolished slavery completely by the early 1800s," but this is simply not true. Indeed, the North never really abolished slavery at all. This term, pertaining to Yankee slavery, is, in truth, a misnomer. What the Northern states actually did was merely suppress the institution until, over time, it naturally faded away due to neglect, unprofitability, and ultimately white racist hostility. This was accomplished through a slow and voluntarily process; one, it should be emphasized, that took place *without any interference from the South.*

This exposes the lie that the Northern states literally "abolished slavery" within their borders on a precise date in a specific year, as our Yankee-biased history books claim. For example: "Vermont in 1777," "Pennsylvania in 1780," "Massachusetts in 1780," "Connecticut in 1784," "Rhode Island in 1784," "New Jersey in 1804," and "New York in 1827."

The fact of the matter is that *none* of the Northern states ever legally ended the institution; they only legislated it into "gradual extinction." This is why a few Yankee states, such as New Hampshire and Delaware, did not fully rid themselves of slavery until the passage of the Thirteenth Amendment, December 6, 1865 (note that the U.S. government continued to allow the enslavement of criminals).

In short, while Pennsylvania, Connecticut, Rhode Island, and New Hampshire all intentionally used a *gradual emancipation plan* (wherein freedom was guaranteed to all persons born in their states after the date of so-called "abolition"), the North as a whole gave herself over 200 leisurely years to eliminate slavery from within her borders. This is hardly what one would describe as "quick and complete abolition," as pro-North historians refer to it.[80]

FACT 64

THE NORTH REFUSED TO GRANT THE SOUTH THE SAME AMOUNT OF TIME TO ABOLISH SLAVERY IN ITS OWN REGION

Thanks to meddlesome Yankee, anti-slavery advocate William Lloyd Garrison of Massachusetts, from 1831 on Northern abolitionists began demanding immediate, complete, and uncompensated emancipation across the South—this coming from the very section of the country that gave birth to both the American slave trade and American slavery!

No one likes to be ordered around, including Southerners; especially not by self-righteous, liberal do-gooders such as Garrison, who have no respect for the rights, ways, and mannerisms of other people, but only simply want to impose their views on those who do not agree with them.

Though the South had been the center of American abolitionism for a half century by this time, she understood that one could not rush the operation.

William L. Garrison.

Complete abolition was a complex procedure that had taken other countries years, decades, centuries, to complete, and it would take Dixie just as long, or longer. Time was needed to prepare, from designing laws and rules to regulate the process of readying 3.5 million former slaves for a life of freedom, to finding the capital ($3 billion, or $57 billion in today's currency) to compensate former slave owners and establish housing and jobs for freedmen and women.

Dixie only asked the North for the same amount of time to develop a functional emancipation program that it had given itself. But this the North would not do. The slavery issue came to be used as a Yankee sledge hammer to force Northern ideas on the South. The South resisted, claiming states' rights under the U.S. Constitution. The North ignored her, and as Lincoln disingenuously said, "the war came."[81]

FACT 65

THE NORTH DOESN'T WANT YOU TO KNOW THAT THE NORTH DID NOT ABOLISH SLAVERY FOR HUMANITARIAN REASONS

Although there were a myriad of reasons why slavery was gradually and officially extinguished in the Northern states, not one of them had to do with humanitarian or civil rights concerns about slaves themselves. The worldly Victorian Yankee felt no apprehension, shame, or guilt for engaging in the "sin" of slavery. Thus when it came time to destroy it he was motivated by reasons of an entirely practical nature, all which can be pared down to three primary factors.

The first reason the North wanted to rid itself of slavery was that it eventually became unprofitable (the same reason Europe finally abolished it). And slavery became unprofitable in the American North, in great part, due to the regions's largely rocky sandy soil, hilly terrain, and short cool summers, all which made it unsuitable for large-scale farming.

Second, there was the North's enormous distance from both Africa (where slaves were picked up) and the tropics (where slaves were needed on sugar, coffee, cotton, pineapple, tobacco, and indigo plantations). This made it much more profitable to sell slaves in, to, and from the American South (which was a shorter distance from both Africa and the Caribbean) than transport them back up to, for example, Rhode Island.

Third, along with the North's growing blue-collar demographic (which made Northern slavery more and more redundant) came increasing racial intolerance toward non-whites. As early as the late 1700s white Northerners "were frankly stating an antipathy of their people toward negroes in any capacity whatever." This, of course, now made abolition in the North absolutely essential, especially economically. Yankee John Adams of Massachusetts, who was to become America's second president two years later, wrote the following in a personal letter dated March 21, 1795:

> Argument might have some weight in the abolition of slavery in the Massachusetts, but the real cause was the multiplication of labouring white people, who would no longer suffer the rich to employ these sable rivals so much to their injury. This principle has kept negro slavery out of France, England, and other parts of Europe. The common people would not suffer the labour, by which alone they could obtain a subsistence, to be done by slaves. . . . The common white people, or rather the labouring people, were the cause of rendering negroes unprofitable servants. Their scoffs and insults, their continual insinuations, filled the negroes with discontent, made them lazy, idle, proud, vicious, and at length wholly useless to their masters, to such a degree that the abolition of slavery became a measure of economy.

Here we have the most significant factor leading to the death of Northern slavery: *Northern white racism*. Most 18th- and 19th-Century Yanks simply preferred living in an all-white society, free from the "naturally disgusting" presence of the black man, as Lincoln and other white racist Northerners expressed it.

Northern blacks who would not leave the U.S. voluntarily were often forced to under the threat of violence. Here a group of African-Americans at one of New York City's ship ports is being coerced, at the tip of a whip, to board a waiting clipper bound for Liberia.

It was this very sentiment which gave birth to the bigoted American Colonization Society, a popular Yankee black deportation organization founded in 1816 in Washington, D.C., by a Northerner, New Jerseyan Robert Finley—and supported by thousands of liberal Northerners. Among them were Lincoln, Harriet Beecher Stowe (author of *Uncle Tom's Cabin*), Horace Greeley (owner of the *New York Tribune*), William Lloyd Garrison (founder of *The Liberator*), Jared Sparks (president of Harvard University), Henry Rutgers (after whom Rutgers University is named), and Edward Everett (after whom the city of Everett, Massachusetts, is named), as well as many other Yanks of note.[82]

FACT 66

THE NORTH DOESN'T WANT YOU TO KNOW THAT THE SOUTH WAS WORKING ON PLANS TO END SLAVERY WHEN LINCOLN ILLEGALLY & UNNECESSARILY INVADED DIXIE

Beginning in the 1600s we have numerous records of Southerners seeking the abolition of both the slave trade and slavery. Indeed, the American abolition movement got its start in the South, in Virginia, to be exact, where, in 1655, the first voluntary emancipation in the American colonies took place. Virginia, of course, is the birthplace of some the South's most famous abolitionists, among them George Washington, Thomas Jefferson, James Madison, and George Mason.

By the early 1800s the American abolition movement was at its peak across Dixie, and we have already seen that of the 130 abolition societies established before 1827 by Northern abolitionist Benjamin Lundy, over 100 (four-fifths of the total membership) were in the South. Southern Quakers too were among the first to come out against the spread of the institution.

Besides North Carolina's noted antislavery leaders, Benjamin Sherwood Hedrick and Daniel Reaves Goodlow, in South Carolina there were the celebrated Quaker sisters Sarah and Angelina Grimké, just two among millions of Southerners fighting for the cause of abolition. The Southern abolition movement involved so many Southerners, so many Southern states, and covered such a large span of time, that the latter Grimké sister wrote an entire book on the subject.

On August 14, 1776, South Carolina rice planter and slave owner Henry Laurens wrote the following to his son John, who was also antislavery:

> You know, my dear son, I abhor slavery. I was born in a country in which slavery had been established by British Parliaments and the

laws of the country for ages before my existence. I found the Christian religion and slavery growing under the same authority and cultivation. I nevertheless dislike it. In former days there was no combating the prejudices of men, supported by interest [money]. The day I hope is approaching when from principles of gratitude and justice every man will strive to be foremost in complying with the golden rule. £20,000 sterling [about £2.5 million, or $4 million in today's currency] would my negroes produce if sold at auction tomorrow. I am not the man who enslaved them; they are indebted to Englishmen for that favour. Nevertheless I am devising means for manumitting many of them and for cutting off the entail of slavery.

What our Yankee biased history books do not teach is that from the 1600s on, every year thousands of Southerners simply emancipated their slaves, and at great financial loss—all without any prompting from the North. Among them were slave owners like Nathan Bedford Forrest, who freed his slaves even before Lincoln's War in 1861,[83] and Robert E. Lee, who liberated his wife's servants before the Emancipation Proclamation was issued in 1863.[84] Unlike in the North, there were no laws against manumission in Dixie, so Southerners gave full vent to their humanitarian instincts.

A Southern planter freeing his slaves years before Lincoln's phony Emancipation Proclamation.

Arguably the South's greatest abolitionist was Thomas Jefferson, who had been working on Southern abolition from his first days as an American statesmen, and who was responsible for prohibiting the American slave trade after the year 1808 (tragically, Yankee slave traders ignored the ban, continuing to sail to Africa right into the Civil War period). Indeed, it was Jefferson's criticism of Britain for imposing slavery on the 13 original American colonies that helped instigate the American Revolution,[85] which in turn led directly to the first "Confederate States of America"—as the USA was known in the 1700s and 1800s.[86] The South was still struggling with precisely how to initiate full abolition, or what Jefferson aptly compared to holding "a wolf behind the ears," when Lincoln tricked the South into firing the first shot of his war at the Battle of Fort Sumter on April 12, 1861.[87]

FACT 67

THE NORTH DOESN'T WANT YOU TO KNOW THAT THE AMERICAN SOUTH WAS THE LAST REGION IN THE WEST TO PRACTICE SLAVERY & THE FIRST TO TRY TO ABOLISH IT

The American abolition movement got its start in the South, in the state of Virginia, where slave owners were already liberating their servants nearly 125 years before the formation of the United States. One of America's most enthusiastic abolitionists, Virginian Thomas Jefferson, rightly compared the difficulty of complete emancipation to holding a wolf by the ears—a fact quite beyond the minds of even the most educated Yankees.

In 1749 Georgia became the last of the 13 British-American colonies to legalize slavery. This was long after every Western nation had already adopted the institution. Seventeen years earlier, in 1732, Georgia became the first colony to place a prohibition against commercial trafficking in slaves into her state constitution, making the American South the first Western region to move toward abolition.

Around the same time, dozens of abolition societies began to spring up across Dixie, with Virginia leading the way in white America's tireless attempt to end slavery—which began in the Dominion State with, as noted, the first voluntary emancipation in 1655.[88]

FACT 68

THE NORTH DOESN'T WANT YOU TO KNOW THAT THERE WERE TENS OF THOUSANDS OF AFRICAN-AMERICAN SLAVE OWNERS

Liberal historians carefully hide the fact from the general public, but the reality is that there were tens of thousands of black slave owners in early America, most who were not counted in the U.S. Census (Census takers were prone to vastly underreporting blacks, free and enslaved). Additionally, some black slaveholders abused and whipped their African servants, another fact that you will seldom find in pro-North, anti-South history books.

These black slaves are working the cotton field of their African-American owner, a free black planter in Mississippi. In nearby Louisiana the Metoyers, an affluent African-American family, owned some 400 black slaves, worth the equivalent of $20 million in today's currency.

In 1830 some 3,700 free Southern blacks owned nearly 12,000 black slaves, an average of almost four slaves a piece. That same year in the Deep South alone nearly 8,000 slaves were owned by some 1,500 black slave owners (about five slaves apiece). In Charleston, South Carolina, as another example, between the years 1820 and 1840, 75 percent of the city's free blacks owned slaves. Furthermore, *25 percent of all free American blacks owned slaves, South and North.*

It is important to remember that in 1861 the South's 300,000 white slave owners made up only 1 percent of the total U.S. white population of 30 million people. Thus, while only one Southern white out of every 300,000 owned slaves (1 percent), one Southern black out of every four owned slaves (25 percent). In other words, far more Southern blacks owned black (and sometimes white) slaves than Southern whites did: 25 percent compared to 1 percent.

Most Southern black slave owners were not only proslavery, they were also pro-South, supporting the Confederate Cause during Lincoln's War as fervently as any white Southerner did. At church each Sunday thousands of blacks would pray for those blacks, both their own slaves and their free friends, who wore the Rebel uniform. Their supplications were simple: they asked God to help all African-American Confederates kill as many Yankees as possible, then return home safely.

One of America's thousands of wealthy black slave owners. Many possessed white slaves as well.

Wealthy blacks bought, sold, and exploited black slaves for profit, just as white slave owners did. The well-known Anna Kingsley, who began life—as was nearly always the case—as a slave in her native Africa, ended up in what is now Jacksonville, Florida, where she became one of early America's many black plantation owners and slaveholders.

Some, like the African-American Metoyers, an anti-abolition family from Louisiana, owned huge numbers of black slaves; in their case, at least 400. At about $1,500 a piece, their servants were worth a total of $600,000, or $20 million in today's currency. This made the Metoyers among the wealthiest people in the U.S., black or white, then or now. Louisiana's all-black Confederate army unit, the Augustin Guards, was named after the family patriarch, Augustin Metoyer.[89]

FACT 69

THE NORTH DOESN'T WANT YOU TO KNOW THAT THERE WERE TENS OF THOUSANDS OF NATIVE-AMERICAN SLAVE OWNERS

Black slavery was not just common among blacks. It was also found among America's 19th-Century Indians, who bought and sold African chattel right alongside black and white slave owners. In fact, one of the many reasons so many Native-Americans sided with the Southern Confederacy was that she promised to enforce the constitutional fugitive slave law in Indian Territory, making it a legal requirement to return runaway slaves to their original Indian owners.

Cheyenne Chief Wolf Robe. The vast majority of Indian peoples practiced slavery, including the Cheyenne—not only on fellow Native-Americans, but later on European-Americans as well.

While the average white slave owner owned five or less slaves (often only one or two), the average red slaveholder owned six. One Choctaw slaver owned 227. Again, it was *non-white* slave owners who individually owned the most slaves, not whites.

Slavery was practiced right up until the 1950s by some Native-American tribes, principally the Haida and the Tlingit peoples of the Pacific Northwest. Among the Haida, slaves performed all of the menial labor, ate only food scraps, were refused health care, and could not own property. And since there were no laws of protection, Haida slaves could be purchased, sold, beaten, molested, and even murdered at the whim of their owners. This is *true* slavery, the exact opposite of the much milder servitude experienced by Africans in the Old American South.[90]

FACT 70

THE NORTH DOESN'T WANT YOU TO KNOW THAT AS "SLAVES" GO, SOUTHERN BLACKS HAD THE HIGHEST STANDARD OF LIVING IN THE WORLD

Southern servitude functioned much like a social welfare program with built-in, lifelong health care and life insurance, operating in some ways like an early form of socialism. Yes, servants helped defray these costs through their work and through monthly percentage payments to their employers. But they earned wages at the same time as well, both via their regular work and also from their personal extracurricular labors.

In all, most Southern slaves were so highly indulged and protected by their owners that *being a "slave" came to be an enviable status symbol among many blacks.* Such bold facts have forced even the most South-loathing, biased historians to admit an obvious truth: *Southern servants were treated far better than servants in*

Southern plantations were not the hellacious "prisons of exploitation and violence" long depicted by anti-South writers. Indeed, with free lifelong room and board, medical care, and education, and countless laws shielding African-Americans from abuse, it is a fact that no servant class in world history has been treated so equitably as the Old South's black "slaves." This is just one reason, among many, that at least 95 percent of blacks remained in Dixie after the Emancipation Proclamation was issued.

any other part of the New World, including the American North.

Would servile blacks have given all these benefits up for freedom? Some would have, and some certainly did. But, after contemplating the quasi-freedom of living in the North, where the anti-African Black Codes were strictly enforced and where white racism was more deeply entrenched, many Southern blacks reconsidered.

When Lincoln's War came, this group, most of whom were third, fourth, and fifth generation Southern-Americans, quite consciously chose to remain in the South, in their own homes, on the plantations with their "white families." Then, when "Honest Abe" freed them, and he and the North tried to deport them back to Africa, with one voice this group cried "no!" For they quite rightly considered themselves true Americans and true Southerners.

After all, by 1860, 99 percent of all blacks were native-born Americans, a larger percentage than for whites. Thus former Southern servant Booker T. Washington wrote: "I was born in the South. I have lived and labored in the South. I wish to be buried in the South."[91]

Virginia-born Booker T. Washington was a true "son of the South," a concept inexplicable to most non-Southerners, but readily understandable to nearly all Southerners, whatever their race, background, or creed.

In the Old South the slave had hundreds of rights, was well respected and even loved by his "master," and was usually accepted as a member of the owner's family. In this illustration, fun-loving servants attend a weekly shindig on the plantation known as a "slave ball," complete with music, food, dancing, and guests from neighboring farms.

FACT 71

THE NORTH DOESN'T WANT YOU TO KNOW THAT FEW CONFEDERATE GENERALS OWNED SLAVES & MOST WERE ABOLITIONISTS

Lee visiting the grave of another famous non-slave owning Confederate general: Stonewall Jackson. Scallywags and Yankees continue to wrongly teach that both men were "slaveholders." It is true that Lee and Jackson had slaves in their homes, and these African-Americans were listed in the Census as such. However, neither of them personally purchased these servants. All were either given to them or the slaves themselves asked to live in their homes due to the generals' charitable natures.

The vast majority of Southerners, as well as Confederate militiamen and politicians, were longtime advocates of not only abolition, but of black enlistment as well. One of these was General Robert E. Lee, across the South still one of the most beloved and highly regarded Confederate officers.

On December 27, 1856, five years before Lincoln's War, Lee—who unlike General Grant and many other Northern officers, never owned slaves in the literal or technical sense, and who had always been opposed to slavery—wrote a letter to his wife Mary Anna in which he stated that slavery is a "moral and political evil," worse even for the white race than for the black race.[92]

Lee's sentiment is just what one would expect from a Virginian, the state where the American abolition movement began, and whose native sons, most notably U.S. Presidents George Washington and Thomas Jefferson, struggled for so long to rid America of the institution; and this while the North was sending hundreds of slave ships to Africa, and whose main port cities, like New York, Providence, Philadelphia, Baltimore, and Boston, were functioning as the literal epicenters of slave trading in the Western hemisphere.

But Lee was far from being the first prominent Confederate to advocate emancipation and the recruitment of Southern blacks. Another example was my cousin Confederate General Pierre G. T. Beauregard, the "Hero of Fort Sumter" and co-designer of the Confederate Battle Flag.

Yet another important Southerner was Louisiana governor and commander-in-chief Thomas O. Moore, who, on March 24, 1862, commissioned the first black militia in the Confederacy (the Native Guards of Louisiana). Moore called on the all-black unit, one that had already been protecting New Orleans for several months, to "maintain their organization, and . . . hold themselves prepared for such orders as may be transmitted to them." Their purpose? To guard homes, property, and Southern rights against "the pollution of a ruthless [Northern] invader."

Another noteworthy pro-black white Confederate officer was General Patrick R. Cleburne, known as the "Stonewall Jackson of the West" for his bold tactics on the battlefield. A native of Ireland and a division commander in the Army of Tennessee, at an officers' meeting on January 2, 1864, the Irishman disclosed a written proposal that would soon become known as the "Cleburne Memorial." Calling for the immediate enlistment and training of black soldiers, it promised complete emancipation for *all* Southern slaves at the end of the War. This was one year before Lincoln issued what he called his "military emancipation," the Emancipation Proclamation—one of whose main purposes was to recruit freed blacks.

Confederate General Patrick R. Cleburne died from Yankee fire (at the Battle of Franklin II) before seeing his dream of black enlistment realized.

In early 1865 Southern Congressman Ethelbert Barksdale stated before the House that *every* Confederate soldier, whatever his rank, wanted and supported black enlistment. This sentiment was backed up by such establishments as the renowned Virginia Military Institute, which agreed, if called upon, to train Southern blacks in the art of soldiering.[93]

FACT 72

The North Doesn't Want You to Know that Many Union Generals, like Ulysses S. Grant, Owned Slaves & Said They Would Not Fight for Abolition

Thousands of Yankees are known to have owned slaves right up to and through Lincoln's War. Among them were the families of Union General George H. Thomas, Union Admiral David G. Farragut, Union General Winfield Scott, and the family of Lincoln's wife, Mary Todd.

Arguably the most famous Yankee slaveholder was Union General Ulysses S. Grant, an Ohioan who evinced no sympathy for the situation of American blacks, never discussed the Underground Railroad, and as an officer in the Mexican War, was waited on by servants—one, a Mexican man named Gregorio, whom he took home with him after the War to entertain his family. Grant never showed any personal interest in his colored servants—except perhaps those who attended him while he was slowly dying in New York in 1885.

Upon his marriage to Julia Boggs Dent in 1848, Grant inherited a small army of 30 black Maryland slaves that belonged to her family. Later, in 1858, he was known to still own "three or four slaves, given to his wife by her father," Colonel Frederick Dent. Grant leased several additional slaves and personally purchased at least one, a 35 year old black man named William Jones. Never once did he reveal a desire to free either his own slaves or Julia's. Instead, like his wife, and most other Northerners at the time, Grant assumed that the white race was superior to non-white races, and that this was simply the natural order of things.

On the eve of Lincoln's War in early 1861, Grant grew increasingly excited over the possibility that a conflict with the South would greatly depreciate black labor, then, he happily exclaimed, "the nigger will never disturb this country again." In an 1862 letter to his father Jesse Root Grant, General Grant wrote honestly:

> I have no hobby of my own with regard to the negro, either to effect his freedom or to continue his bondage.

This apathy for the black man continued throughout Lincoln's War. In 1863 Grant penned: "I never was an abolitionist, not even what could be called anti-slavery." Even after the issuance of Lincoln's Emancipation Proclamation Grant maintained the same sentiment, noting sourly that white Americans were now still "just as free to avoid the social intimacy with the blacks as ever they were . . ."

Union General Ulysses S. Grant was an authentic slave owner, one who leased, purchased, and sold slaves before, during, and even after the War had ended. He was only stopped by the Thirteenth Amendment in December 1865.

Since Lincoln's bogus and illicit Emancipation Proclamation on January 1, 1863, did not liberate slaves in the North (or anywhere else, for that matter), Grant was permitted to keep his black chattel—which is precisely what he did. In fact, he did not free them until he was forced to by the passage of the Thirteenth Amendment on December 6, 1865, which occurred eight months *after* Lincoln's death and the War had ended.

And what or who was behind the Thirteenth Amendment? It was not Grant, Lincoln, Greeley, Garrison, or any other Northerner. It was proposed by a *Southern* man, John Henderson of Missouri.

But the amendment seemed to have little meaning to Grant or his wife Julia, the latter, who as late as 1876, still looked upon all blacks as slaves. We should not be shocked by any of this. It was the celebrated Yankee General Grant who, in the midst of Lincoln's War, said that the only purpose of the conflict was to "restore the union," and if he ever found out it was for abolition he would immediately defect to the other side and join the Confederacy.[94]

144 ∾ THE GREAT YANKEE COVERUP

FACT 73

THE NORTH DOESN'T WANT YOU TO KNOW THAT THE CONFEDERATE MILITARY WAS MULTIRACIAL, MULTICULTURAL, & MULTIETHNIC

We have been taught that the Confederate armies were "100 percent white," this due to the "boundless white racism" that existed across the Old South. We have already seen that the integrated South was far less racist than the segregated North, so it is obvious that this charge cannot be true. The South's army and navy, in fact, reflected the region's citizenship, which was made up of every race, creed, and nationality.

Though, thanks to the vicious Yankee custom of burning down Southern courthouses, exact statistics are impossible to come by, Southern historians have determined that the following numbers are basically accurate. In descending numerical order the Confederate army and navy was composed of about 1 million European-Americans, 300,000 to 1 million African-Americans, 70,000 Native-Americans, 60,000 Latin-Americans, 50,000 foreigners, 12,000 Jewish-Americans, and 10,000 Asian-Americans.

A group of Cherokee Confederate veterans, gathered for a Confederate reunion in New Orleans, Louisiana, in 1903. An estimated 70,000 Indians fought for the Confederacy, primarily members from the Cherokee, Choctaw, Chickasaw, Seminole, Osage, and Creek tribes. Despite being outnumbered three to one, thousands of European-Americans, African-Americans, Native-Americans, Latin-Americans, Asian-Americans, Jewish-Americans, and foreigners combined to create a Confederate force so powerful that it was able to hold off the Union army and navy for four years. The Confederate military was simply a mirror image of Dixie's multiracial, multiethnic, multicultural society. Pro-North advocates do not want you to know any of this, of course, which is why they have withheld these facts from you, and it is why they will withhold them from your children and your grandchildren.

True Southerners, of all races, continue to be proud of our region's multiracial history, and of the many contributions made to Dixie by individuals of all colors, religions, and nations.[95]

This photograph destroys two Yankee fictions simultyaneously: 1) that Southern whites and blacks detested one another, and 2) that there was no such thing as a black Confederate soldier. Andrew Martin Chandler (left) and one of his family's servants, Silas Chandler (right), are shown here in official Confederate uniforms, full fledged soldiers in the 44th Mississippi Infantry. Armed to the teeth in preparation for the fight against the illicit Northern invaders, such brave young men, white and black, were prepared to face death side-by-side if need be. This type of interracial pairing was repeated hundreds of thousands of times across the South during Lincoln's War. While Dixie's black servants were sometimes ordered to go into battle to accompany white loved ones, just as often they went of their own accord, anxious to put on Confederate gray and show "Marse Linkum" who was boss.

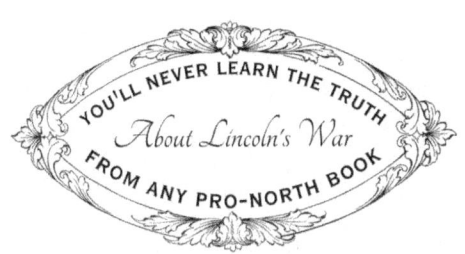

FACT 74

THE NORTH DOESN'T WANT YOU TO KNOW THAT IN 1860 A MERE 4.8 PERCENT OF SOUTHERNERS OWNED SLAVES

Pro-North writers would have us believe that "every Southerner was once a slave owner." However, the opposite is true. In 1860 the South had reached its highest rate of slave ownership. According to the U.S. Census that year, with a white population of 7,215,525, only 4.8 percent, or 385,000, of all Southerners owned slaves, the other 95.2 percent did not. Of those that did, most owned less than five.

Correcting for the mistakes of Census takers—which would include counting slave-hirers as slave owners and counting more than once those thousands of slave owners who annually moved the same slaves back and forth across multiple states—this figure, 4.8 percent, is no doubt too large. Either way, at the time Southerners themselves believed that only about 5 percent of their number owned slaves, which is slightly high, but roughly correct.[96]

Field hands running a cotton gin on an Alabama plantation. Slave owning was almost solely a rich man's business, which is why, contrary to Yankee myth, at slavery's peak in the antebellum South in 1860, only 4.8 percent of white adult males owned black servants. Southern historian Shelby Foote rightly called the other 95.2 percent "the slaveless majority," a reality never discussed by liberal university professors, never noted by the left-wing media, and never mentioned by pro-North writers.

FACT 75

THE NORTH DOESN'T WANT YOU TO KNOW THAT ANTEBELLUM YANKEES VIEWED SLAVERY AS THE "CORNERSTONE OF THE UNION"

Anti-South writers enjoy excoriating Confederate Vice President Alexander H. Stephens for his March 21, 1861, speech at Savannah, Georgia, in which he made this infamous statement:

> [The] corner-stone [of the Constitution of the Southern Confederacy] rests upon the great truth, that the negro is not equal to the white man; that slavery, subordination to the superior race, is his natural and normal condition.

Before discussing the facts behind these words, let us compare them with those of Yankee President Abraham Lincoln, delivered publicly a few years earlier on July 17, 1858, at Springfield, Illinois:

> My declarations upon this subject of negro slavery may be misrepresented, but cannot be misunderstood. I have said that I do not understand the Declaration [of Independence] to mean that all men were created equal in all respects. . . . Certainly the negro is not our equal in color—perhaps not in many other respects . . .

A few months later, on September 18, 1858, at Charleston, Illinois, Lincoln made the following statement:

> I will say then that I am not, nor ever have been, in favor of bringing about in any way the social and political equality of the white and black races—that I am not, nor ever have been, in favor of making voters or jurors of negroes, nor of qualifying them to hold office, nor to intermarry with white people; and I will say in addition to this that there is a physical difference between the white and black races which I believe will forever forbid the two races living together on terms of social and political equality. And inasmuch as

they cannot so live, while they do remain together there must be the position of superior and inferior, and I as much as any other man am in favor of having the superior position assigned to the white race.

Our point here is that Vice President Stephens' racism was no different than President Lincoln's. Both men were products of a 19th-Century white society that saw blacks as an "inferior race," as Lincoln always referred to African-Americans. Thus, if critics of the South wish to avoid being called hypocrites, Northerner Lincoln must be denounced just as heartily as Southerner Stephens. As the "Great Emancipator" Lincoln himself said of "nearly all white people" living in America at the time:

> There is a natural disgust in the minds of nearly all white people, to the idea of an indiscriminate amalgamation of the white and black races.

As for Stephens' words, they turn out to be far less venomous and racist than modern South-loathers have asserted—and in fact Stephens was widely known as a true friend of the black man.[97] For one thing, the Vice President was engaging in hyperbole to get his point across, a common enough practice among politicians. Second, the speech we read today is not a literal translation of the original, but an "interpretation" by journalists in the audience, who introduced their own biases and mistakes into the final transcription. Third, Stephens himself repeatedly maintained that his words had been misinterpreted, and for good reason. When he made his comment about slavery being the "cornerstone" of American society, he was merely repeating the words of a *Yankee* judge, Associate Justice of the U.S. Supreme Court, Henry Baldwin of Connecticut who, 28 years earlier, in 1833, had said:

> Slavery is the corner-stone of the [U.S.] Constitution. The foundations of the Government are laid and rest on the rights of property in slaves, and the whole structure must fall by disturbing the corner-stone.[98]

As Richard M. Johnston noted later in 1884, all Stephens did during his "Cornerstone Speech" was accurately point out the fact that "on the subject of slavery there was no essential change in the new [Southern Confederate] Constitution from the old [the U.S. Constitution]."[99]

FACT 76

THE NORTH DOESN'T WANT YOU TO KNOW THAT FEW SLAVES ACTUALLY USED THE UNDERGROUND RAILROAD & THAT IT WAS CONSIDERED A FAILURE BY MOST ABOLITIONISTS

The Underground Railroad was not the gargantuan, tightly organized, national antislavery system that pro-North writers claim it to have been. Though it functioned throughout most of the War, only about 2,000 slaves (just 500 servants a year) out of 4.5 million (North and South) availed themselves of it—a mere 0.04 percent of the total.

According to scholarly studies, few antebellum Southern slaves used the Railroad: the fugitive slaves that passed through New York, for instance, all came from Maryland and Delaware, non-Southern states. Black Southern escapees preferred staying in Dixie, simply disappearing into the anonymity of the big Southern cities where they easily merged with the large free black population. (This is not surprising: even after Lincoln's Final Emancipation Proclamation was issued, 95 percent of all Southern slaves voluntarily stayed at home in Dixie.)

It is telling that the definitive early source on the "rail," William Still's 1872 book, *The Underground Railroad: A Record of Facts, Authentic Narratives, Letters, Etc.*, features not millions, not thousands, not even hundreds, but a mere handful of black slaves who were, as the author phrases it, "plucked from the jaws of slavery" via this particular method. And nearly all of these testimonials are of single individuals, with the exception of a few rare slave groups, usually comprising no more than four to six people.

In the end, as nearly all enslaved American blacks seeking freedom did so on their own and without any assistance, the so-called "Underground Railroad" was little more than a morale booster for abolitionists, as opposed to an actual effective escape system for slaves.[100]

FACT 77

THE NORTH DOESN'T WANT YOU TO KNOW THAT THE CONFEDERATE STATES OF AMERICA WAS NOT A "SLAVE REGIME"

The Confederate States of America was not a "slave regime" or a "slavocracy," as anti-South partisans have maliciously and incorrectly labeled it. As noted, in 1860 only 4.8 percent of the total white male population of the South owned black servants, and this in the same region where the American abolition movement was born. This is hardly what could be called a "slave regime."

Indians with a freshly captured white female slave.

America did indeed have its slave regimes, but they were not in the South.

The first slavocracies existed among Native-Americans, who enslaved one another as a routine aspect of Indian society, using some of the most brutal and sadistic forms of slavery ever chronicled. After European colonization, Native-Americans began enslaving untold thousands of whites, blacks, and browns as well.

America's greatest slavocracy, however, emerged among the white colonists of the Northeast, where both the American slave trade and American slavery were born in the early 1600s. Of these states, New York came to be "America's Slave Capital," a true slave regime that imported and sold millions of (previously enslaved) Africans over a period of 239 years, far longer than any other state, North or South.[101]

New York was America's only true slavocracy, a 239 year long slave regime without parallel in the annals of Western history.

FACT 78

THE NORTH DOESN'T WANT YOU TO KNOW THAT THE SOUTHERN CONFEDERACY NEVER ENGAGED IN THE SLAVE TRADE

As we have seen, the only American slave ships to ever sail from the U.S. left from Northern ports aboard Northern slave vessels, that were designed by Northern engineers, constructed by Northern shipbuilders, fitted out by Northern riggers, piloted by Northern ship captains, manned by Northern crews, launched from Northern marine ports, funded by Northern businessmen, all which was supported by the vast majority of the anti-abolitionist Northern population.

In other words, the American slave trade was a purely Yankee business, one that operated under the auspices of, not the Confederate Flag, but the U.S. Flag. Yet it is the Confederate Flag that is now associated with slavery. Such has been the overwhelming power of the North's revisionist version of American history that lies, slander, and disinformation concerning the Southern Confederacy have come to be regarded as fact. This is The Great Yankee Coverup.[102]

A Dutch slave ship off-loading African slaves (who had already been enslaved by fellow tribesmen in Africa) at a slave market in New York Harbor. There was no such thing as a Confederate or even a Southern slave ship, slave ship captain, or slave port. All American slaves entered the country aboard either foreign ships or Northern owned vessels operating under the U.S. flag.

FACT 79

THE NORTH DOESN'T WANT YOU TO KNOW THAT THE SOUTHERN CONFEDERACY PLANNED TO END SLAVERY BEFORE THE U.S. DID

In January 1865 Confederate Secretary of State Judah P. Benjamin ordered Confederate commissioner Duncan F. Kenner to England to announce the C.S.'s commitment to full emancipation. This was nearly a year before the U.S. issued the Thirteenth Amendment (on December 6) banning slavery throughout the nation. (Let us note again that, contrary to Yankee mythology, the Northern states *never* officially abolished slavery. Instead they slowly and methodically destroyed the institution through a long drawn out process known as "gradual emancipation," taking over 100 years to complete the process, which finally ended in 1865 with the ratification of the Thirteenth Amendment. Tragically, the North refused to grant the South the same privilege, and instead demanded "immediate abolition," an impossibility at the time.)

The Confederacy's motion to abolish slavery across the South had the complete support of the Southern populace, of course, the very people who had inaugurated the American abolition movement in the early 1700s. One of the better known of the great Southern abolitionists was the celebrated antislavery Virginian, Robert E. Lee, who, on December 27, 1856—five years before Lincoln's War—made this comment about the "peculiar institution":

> There are few, I believe, in this enlightened age, but what will acknowledge that slavery as an institution is a moral and political evil in any country.

Later, during the War, like *all* Southern civilians and Confederate soldiers and officers, Lee supported the idea of immediate abolition and black enlistment, a fact you will never read in any pro-North book.[103]

FACT 80

THE NORTH DOESN'T WANT YOU TO KNOW THAT THE NORTH PRACTICED SLAVERY FOR OVER A CENTURY LONGER THAN THE SOUTH

Southern slavery lasted from 1749, when Georgia became the first Southern state to legalize slavery, to 1865, the year the Thirteenth Amendment was ratified and American slavery was officially abolished, a mere 116 years.

In contrast, Northern slavery lasted from 1641, when Massachusetts became the first Northern state to legalize slavery, to 1865, a span of 224 years. This period increases if we count from 1626, the year New York imported the first black slaves into North America, a span of 239 years—ending in 1865.

Either way, the North practiced slavery for over a century longer than the South did, between 108 and 123 years longer.[104]

The Great Yankee Coverup is meant to hide the facts about American slavery, pretending that it did not originate in their region and that they never practiced the institution. To further obfuscate the truth, the blame for the entire business has been pinned on the South. However, not even the most clever and nefarious anti-South historians can suppress antebellum illustrations like this one, which shows shackled African slaves being marched along in front of the U.S. Capitol Building at Washington, D.C., circa 1836.

FACT 81

THE NORTH DOESN'T WANT YOU TO KNOW THAT THE MAJORITY OF NORTHERNERS WERE ANTI-ABOLITIONISTS

Like Lincoln, the great majority of Northerners, including the Union armies, were anti-abolition and did not support the idea of nationwide emancipation. In fact, abolitionists made up only a tiny but loud and much detested minority in the North, as Lincoln himself was well aware. This is why, after all, they were given the derogatory nickname "radicals."

Proof that the North was not truly an abolitionist area was that while it abolished slavery in its own backyard, the majority still did not want to end slavery in the South, for New England's textile mills, and the New York industrialists who owned them, were still making vast fortunes from Southern cotton, picked and ginned by millions of Southern servants. Thus, a full scale Northern effort began to keep Southern slavery alive, and even strengthen and enlarge it.

It was in this way that when the white North grew tired of dealing with blacks and slavery, she pushed the institution southward on a mostly unwilling populace, one that had been trying to officially abolish it since the early 1700s. For example, when New York slave owner John Bouiness freed one of his black servants in the North, at the same time he also had five other

Lincoln with his son Tad. There is good reason why "Honest Abe" won both presidential elections in the anti-abolitionist, slave trade loving North: he was the only candidate who promised *not* to interfere with slavery, a commitment fully backed by his party, the Republicans (the Liberal Party of the day).

slaves sold in Virginia.

It has been estimated that at least 99 percent of Yankee businessmen were anti-abolitionists who supported the continuation of Southern slavery, for, as mentioned, the cotton that Southern slaves produced was one of the North's largest financial assets. Among the most vociferous of this group were New York's "Wall Street Boys," which had bankrolled Lincoln's first (and later his second) presidential campaign using money they had made primarily from the Yankee slave trade. There was also the Boston elite, who made it known that they were quite willing to make huge concessions to the South in the interest of making money.

Around 1831 Rhode Islander Elizabeth Buffum Chace and her father Arnold Buffum, the first president of the New England Anti-Slavery Society, decided to travel across their region in order to enlist Yankee support for their emancipation plan. In her 1891 memoir Chace writes:

> I remember well, how eager we were, in our revived Anti-Slavery zeal, to present the cause of the slave to everybody we met [in New England]; not doubting that, when their attention was called to it, they would be ready, as we were, to demand his immediate emancipation. But, alas! their commercial relations, their political associations, and with many, their religious fellowship with the people of the South, so blinded the eyes, hardened the hearts and stifled the consciences of the North, that we found very few people who were ready to give any countenance or support to the new AntiSlavery movement.

Is it any wonder then that the 1860 Republican Party Platform contained paragraphs promising to leave the "peculiar institution" alone, while declaring that Republicans were only against the extension of slavery, not slavery itself? That in his First Inaugural Address, March 4, 1861, Lincoln pledged not to disturb slavery? Or that American slavery did not come to a final end until December 6, 1865 (eight months after Lincoln's death), with the passage of the Thirteenth Amendment?

Here we have more evidence, if more is needed, that the Civil War was not a contest over slavery. It was, in great part, a *Northern* contest over slavery money, a *Southern* contest over constitutional rights (that is, self-determination).[105]

FACT 82

THE NORTH DOESN'T WANT YOU TO KNOW THAT THE MOST DANGEROUS LEG OF AN AFRICAN SLAVE'S JOURNEY WAS NOT THE MIDDLE PASSAGE, BUT THE BEGINNING AFRICAN PASSAGE

While there is no doubt that the oceangoing Middle Passage was indeed horrendous in many ways, it was not the most hazardous or unpleasant leg of an African slave's journey through the notorious Slave Triangle, as pro-North writers insist. It was the harrowing overland Beginning Passage, the land route from Africa's interior to the coast—where three times as many slaves died as on the Middle Passage.

An African slave was far more likely to die on the Beginning Passage, the land route from Africa's interior to the coast, than on the Middle Passage, the oceangoing journey from the coast to the American Northeast. The Great Yankee Coverup has suppressed this fact.

This was due not just to the shock of capture, but also to exhaustion, hyperthermia, malnourishment, sleep deprivation, dehydration, illness, animal attacks, and the inevitable physical abuse suffered at the hands of their tyrannical African captors. All of this made the misery and the mortality rates of the Middle Passage—which were after all, as one historian noted, merely part of "the then customary dangers and hardships of the sea"—pale in comparison.

Most importantly, let us note here that the oceangoing Middle Passage was operated by European and American whites, while the overland Beginning Passage, part of the domestic African slavery system, was run and controlled strictly by Africans.[106]

FACT 83

THE NORTH DOESN'T WANT YOU TO KNOW THAT YANKEE SLAVE SHIPS WERE SAILING TO AFRICA RIGHT INTO THE CIVIL WAR PERIOD

As proof we have the example of Captain Nathaniel Gordon of New York, the only American ever tried, convicted, and executed for slaving. His death occurred on February 21, 1862, at President Lincoln's personal order.

More evidence comes from the *Nightingale*, the last American slave ship to be captured by the U.S. government. The New York slaver was confiscated on April 21, 1861. Known fondly to Northerners as the "Prince of Slavers," the *Nightingale* was built in Maine, fitted out in New Hampshire, sailed from Massachusetts, and had a New York captain.

At the time of her seizure, this vessel, from the so-called "abolitionist North," had nearly 1,000 manacled Africans on board. She was doing "business as usual" up until the first few weeks of the Civil War, all the while proudly flying the U.S. flag from her mast.[107]

The notorious U.S. slave ship Nightingale had a purely Northern provenance. Constructed in Maine and outfitted in New Hampshire, she sailed from Massachusetts under the command of a New York captain. With some 1,000 African slaves in her hull, in 1861 she became famous for being the last slave ship to be seized by the U.S. government. Note the large U.S. flag flying from her stern.

FACT 84

THE NORTH DOESN'T WANT YOU TO KNOW THAT NEARLY 100 PERCENT OF SOUTHERN BLACKS SUPPORTED THE CONFEDERACY

Of the South's 3.5 million black servants, the "vast majority," 95 percent (19 out of 20), remained in the South, all the while maintaining their loyalty to Dixie. Ignoring Lincoln's fake proclamation of freedom, they instead pledged their allegiance to their home states, to the South, and to their white families. Remaining at home they ran their owner's farm, grew food, produced provisions for the Confederate military, and protected their master's family and property while he was away on the battlefield. In 1910 Pastor Benjamin F. Riley noted that the Southern black servant

> sustained the armies of the Confederacy during the great Civil War; he was the guardian of the helpless women and children of the South while the husbands and sons were at the distant front doing battle . . .; against him was not a whisper of unfaithfulness or of disloyalty during all this trying and bloody period; when the land was invaded by the [Northern] armies . . . he remained faithful still, and often at great personal risk of life, secreted from the invader [his owner's] . . . horses and mules, and buried the treasures of the family that they might not fall into the hands of the enemies of the whites . . . . he declined to accept freedom when it was offered by the invading army, preferring to remain loyal and steadfast to the charge committed to him by the absent master, all this and more the Negro slave did. There was not a day during the trying period of the Civil War when he might not have disbanded the Southern armies. An outbreak on his part against the defenseless homes of the South would have occasioned the utter dissolution of the Southern armies, and turned the anxious faces of the veterans in gray toward their homes. But no Southern soldier ever dreamed of the possibility of a condition like this. So far as his home was concerned, it was not any apprehension of the unfaithfulness of the slaves which occasioned the slightest alarm.[108]

FACT 85

THE NORTH DOESN'T WANT YOU TO KNOW THAT SLAVERY IS STILL BEING VIGOROUSLY PRACTICED AROUND THE WORLD, INCLUDING IN AFRICA & THE UNITED STATES

Contrary to popular opinion, slavery did not die out after Lincoln's phony Emancipation Proclamation in 1863. The institution continues to thrive and is universal in scope: according to Britain's Anti-Slavery Society, slavery is still found all over the world, even in the U.S., though it continues to flourish most consistently in Africa, the Middle East, the Far East, and in parts of South America.

Not only this, but studies reveal that the rate of slavery is actually increasing not decreasing, for *there are now more slaves in the world than at any other time in human history*: in 1933, 5 million slaves were estimated to exist around the globe. Yet, at the time of this writing, 2015, at least 30 million people are currently living under authentic slavery, while an additional 200 million people worldwide are suffering under one type of bondage or another.

African-owned slaves in present day Africa, a not uncommon sight. Slavery is on the rise worldwide.

Let us contrast these figures with the Old South, which never possessed more than 3.5 million servants (not true "slaves"), 86 percent of these, in 1860, which were American born.

As for the U.S., according to a pre-2000 CIA study, 50,000 people (mostly women and children) were enslaved in the U.S. At the time of this survey, this number was expected to rise—and indeed it has. As of 2013 there were 60,000 slaves in the U.S. Both these slaves and their enslavers come in every race and color, more proof that slavery—whether modern, Victorian, Medieval, ancient, or prehistoric—is not, and never has been, based on skin color.[109]

SECTION FOUR

DAVIS & LINCOLN

African authorities, like this Susu chief and his staff, were responsible for the enslavement of thousands of fellow Africans, a reality now ignored by mainstream historians. If the inventors of The Great Yankee Coverup had their way, no one would ever be exposed to the facts concerning indigenous African slavery, which has endured for thousands of years into the present. In 1908 J. Clarence Stonebraker wrote: "[Yankee] slave dealers only obtained their slaves by one [African] tribe conquering another and delivering same into the hands of the slave dealers, or by the consent of parents, getting up their children and selling them. The very false stories that a [slave] vessel's crew could go into the jungles and drive out as many negroes as they wished is grossly vile, and was hatched along with many others by the unconscionable and incorrigible prejudice of [Northern] partisans, and for an equally vile purpose. Such things are still being taught and believed to an extent in the frigid [Yankee] section of our country." In essence, it was African chiefs who first enslaved other Africans, and it was African slave merchants, slave drivers known as *slattees*, who then forcibly marched them to the coast in chains and sold them to Arabs, Europeans, and eventually Yankees. In plain English, up until at least 1820, "no free blacks ever came to America from Africa." Will Africa ever acknowledge the fact that she greatly contributed to, eagerly helped maintain, and actually laid the groundwork for the Atlantic slave trade? Not if the supporters of The Great Yankee Coverup and other members of the anti-South movement have their way.

FACT 86

THE NORTH DOESN'T WANT YOU TO KNOW THAT JEFFERSON DAVIS, NOT ABRAHAM LINCOLN, WAS THE REAL FRIEND OF BLACKS

While Lincoln was plotting the exile of all blacks from America's shores, Confederate President Jefferson Davis and his wife Varina (Howell) adopted a young black boy, Jim Limber, who they raised as their own in the Confederate White House. During the War they always treated their black servants equitably and with the greatest respect, as part of their family in fact. And after Lee's surrender, during the Davis family's escape southward, their coachman was a "faithful" free black.

Authentic history attests that Confederate President Jefferson Davis was a genuine benefactor of African-Americans.

While Lincoln was blocking emancipation, black enlistment, and black civil rights, and working day and night on his colonization plan to deport all blacks out of the U.S., Davis was busy trying to figure out a way to end Southern slavery, enlist blacks, initiate black civil rights, and incorporate blacks into mainstream American society.

Not surprisingly, President Davis' first Confederate states marshal was a black man. Lincoln never appointed a black man to any position, let alone U.S. states marshal, and unquestionably he would have never adopted a black child.

Later, after the War, the one-time Rebel president and his wife sold their plantation, Brierfield, to a former slave. Davis even spoke once of a time when he led "negroes against a lawless body of armed white men . . .," something we can be sure that white separatist Lincoln never did—or would have even considered.

Davis was also against black colonization (preferring that blacks remain in the South, where they had been since the 1500s), banned the foreign slave trade in the Confederacy four years before the Union did, and committed the C.S. to complete abolition in January 1865, almost a year before the U.S. implemented the Thirteenth Amendment.

For these reasons alone it is Davis, not Lincoln, who must be considered the true friend of blacks.[110]

The facts are unimpeachable: Davis was the epitome of racial tolerance compared to Lincoln.

FACT 87

THE NORTH DOESN'T WANT YOU TO KNOW THAT DAVIS WAS BOTH A GREAT MAN & AN AMERICAN PATRIOT

Though South-haters take particular pleasure in deprecating our Confederate president, naturally we take the opposite stance, and for good reason. Jefferson Davis was a West Point graduate, a Mexican War hero, a faithful husband, an outstanding father, an eminent Mississippi senator, a bold defender of the Southern Cause, a talented author, and a fearless and knowledgeable protector of the Constitution.

Also an honest politician and a brave military man who was popular with his soldiers, Davis was an extraordinary leader of the Confederate nation during what was arguably America's most difficult period. In the eyes of the South these things alone make him a great man, and an immortal hero.

The pro-North movement also enjoys painting Davis as a traitor to the United States for accepting the presidency of a region that broke away from the Union. Yet, we have seen, and proven, that secession was—and remains—a legal right as laid down in the Declaration of Independence (1776), the Articles of Confederation (1781), and the U.S. Constitution (1789). This being so, Davis was no traitor. Quite the opposite: he was an outstanding American patriot!

It was big government progressive Abraham Lincoln who betrayed his country by re-interpreting the Constitution to fit his own agenda (like another Liberal, Barack Hussein Obama, who called the Constitution "an imperfect document," Lincoln once said that he did not like the Constitution as it was written), then illegally invaded the lawfully formed Confederate States of America in 1861 (and that without congressional approval). This is why in the traditional South we consider Lincoln the true traitor to the United States.[111]

FACT 88

THE NORTH DOESN'T WANT YOU TO KNOW THAT COMPARED TO LINCOLN, DAVIS WAS THE SUPERIOR PRESIDENT & THE TRUE GREAT EMANCIPATOR

If you are only familiar with the Northern version of the Civil War, you no doubt believe that Davis could not hold a candle to the "Great Emancipator" Abraham Lincoln. Here in the traditional South, however, we maintain that this is a highly subjective myth, one with which we wholeheartedly disagree. Some in Dixie (that is, scallywags) have gone as far as siding with the Yanks in granting Lincoln superior status as a war president. However, this too is debatable and, in our estimation, completely untenable. And here is why.

Lincoln assured a Yankee victory in great part by subverting the Constitution, engaging in political chicanery (such as rigging elections) and countless war crimes (such as waging war without the approval of Congress, arresting and torturing Northern peace advocates, shutting down the legislatures of Northern states, allowing the theft, abuse, rape and murder of countless Southern civilians), disregarding the Geneva Convention (by sanctioning total war on the South), and psychologically and emotionally manipulating the Northern populace.

Davis, on the other hand, helped guarantee Southern defeat by honoring the Confederate Constitution, avoiding political skullduggery, holding his troops to a high standard of behavior, observing the Geneva

Davis, one of the world's most exceptional political leaders, was far superior to Lincoln in morals, ethics, education, intelligence, honor, and principles—which, to a great degree, is precisely why the South lost the War.

Convention, discouraging criminal activity among his soldiers, and being honest with the Southern people.

Without regard to who won or lost the War, which one then was the superior war president? It is clear where we in the traditional South stand, but you the reader must judge for yourself.

Davis launched the beginnings of complete abolition in the South over a year before the North issued the Thirteenth Amendment, making him the true Great Emancipator.

As far as Lincoln being the "Great Emancipator," we will deal with this fairytale in more detail shortly. Suffice it to say that this idea is absurd in the extreme. For Lincoln was what we would today consider a white racist, a white supremacist, and a white separatist. Furthermore, he did not legally or officially free a single American slave during his lifetime (it was eight months after Lincoln's death, in December 1865, that the Thirteenth Amendment finally freed all American slaves).

In truth, it was Davis who was the true Great Emancipator, which is why he is known as such by all enlightened Southerners. For it was Davis who began the official, *and* legal, emancipation of slaves over a year earlier, on November 7, 1864, with the recruitment of Southern blacks into the Confederate military;[112] and it was Davis who, in early 1865, was busy designing plans for full and complete abolition across the South—nearly a year before the ratification of the Thirteenth Amendment in the North.[113]

FACT 89

THE NORTH DOESN'T WANT YOU TO KNOW THE REAL REASON JEFFERSON DAVIS WAS NEVER BROUGHT TO TRIAL

If we are to believe anti-South writers, the *only* reason Davis was never brought to trial after the War was because he was too sickly and cowardly. South-loathers, of course, consider this unfortunate since they believe he should have been punished, even executed, for his "treasonous crimes against the U.S."

Davis at Beauvoir, his home in Mississippi.

The reality is that, at the time, Davis was more than healthy and courageous enough to stand trial. More to the point, he repeatedly requested a trial, but was repeatedly turned down. The U.S. government had asked three different prosecuting attorneys to try him, but all three refused, deeming the case thoroughly unwinnable. Why?

A public trial would have allowed the South's brilliant legal minds, including Davis', to prove the legality of secession *and* expose The Great Yankee Coverup; that is, the concealment of the many illegalities of Lincoln's War. As one of the North's own lawyers stated:

> Gentleman, the Supreme Court of the United States will have to acquit that man under the Constitution when it will be proven to the world that the North waged an unconstitutional warfare against the South.

No wonder that before Davis was captured trying to reorganize his armies, President Lincoln and General Grant had ardently "wished and hoped" that he would escape unnoticed into the Southern wilderness.

The truth is that it was not Davis who committed treason against the U.S. It was Lincoln. And it was Lincoln who, had he lived, should have been tried and punished.[114]

FACT 90

THE NORTH DOESN'T WANT YOU TO KNOW THAT LINCOLN DIDN'T PRESERVE THE UNION, HE DESTROYED IT

Did Lincoln and his total war on the South "preserve the Union"? The North unhesitatingly answers yes. But that does not make it true. Indeed, anything the North says about Lincoln's War must be treated as suspect, for it has invested 150 years and billions of dollars in The Great Yankee Coverup, and is not about to admit its deception.

Even big government politicians, like Founding Father Alexander Hamilton, once acknowledged that the Union cannot be held together by physical force. Unfortunately Lincoln did not.

The South, of course, answers this question with a resounding no, and here the facts are on her side. A union is, by definition, a *voluntary* association. An example of this is Western marriage: the voluntary union of two people. Western law would thus consider a marriage performed under coercion invalid.

The original United States Confederacy (designated by the Founders as such from 1781 to 1789) was designed in the same manner: as a civil marriage; that is, as a voluntary union. This "wedding" formalized the affiliation between its weak decentralized government and the 13-member group of powerful, self-governing, independent nation-states. The Articles of Confederation, and their later replacement, the U.S. Constitution, both upheld the idea of accession and secession: a state could join or leave the Union voluntarily. As in a marital union, one must be able to leave volitionally what one has entered volitionally, which is why both marriage and divorce are legal in the U.S.

In 1861 the South "divorced" the North legally and constitutionally. What Lincoln and his War did was to force, at the end of a rifle barrel, the South to "remarry" the North, in essence voiding their earlier separation. But far from preserving the Union, this illegal "shotgun wedding" destroyed it. How? By forcing one group, against its will, to form an association with another.

In the West there is no such thing as a *legal* involuntary union, civil or political. Like Lincoln's act to "preserve the Union" by force, it is an oxymoron. Even the Liberals among the Founding Fathers understood this elementary concept. In 1788, 73 years before the American "Civil War," for instance, arch anti-Jeffersonian, Alexander Hamilton said insightfully:

> It has been observed, to coerce the States is one of the maddest projects that was ever devised. A failure of compliance will never be confined to a single State. This being the case, can we suppose it wise to hazard a civil war? Suppose Massachusetts, or any large State, should refuse, and Congress should attempt to compel them, would they not have influence to procure assistance, especially from those States which are in the same situation as themselves? What picture does this idea present to our view? A complying State at war with a non-complying State; Congress marching the troops of one State in to the bosom of another; this State collecting auxiliaries, and forming, perhaps, a majority against its Federal head. Here is a nation at war with itself. Can any reasonable man be well disposed towards a Government which makes war and carnage the only means of supporting itself—a Government that can exist only by the sword? Every such war must involve the innocent with the guilty. This single consideration should be sufficient to dispose every peaceable citizen against such a Government. But can we believe that one State will ever suffer itself to be used as an instrument of coercion? The thing is a dream; it is impossible.

Unfortunately for the American people, Lincoln turned what Hamilton called an "impossible dream" into a possible nightmare: under Lincoln the USA became an involuntary union that exists "only by the sword"—the opposite of that intended by the Founding generation. Here in the South we do not consider this "preserving the Union." We call it what it is: the destruction of the Union.[115]

FACT 91

THE NORTH DOESN'T WANT YOU TO KNOW THAT LINCOLN WAS NOT ONLY AN AGNOSTIC BUT AN ANTI-CHRISTIAN

The Pro-North movement would like us to think that Lincoln was a Bible-believing, God-fearing Christian with the heart of a saint. Actually he only passed himself off as a "good Christian" when it benefitted him politically.

The truth is that he was a skeptic, a humanist, and an "infidel," one who opposed organized religion, told impious stories, mocked Christian revivals, never prayed, never attended church, never joined any religious faith or denomination, never opened a Bible, never mentioned Jesus, and was well-known for his lack of belief in the divinity of Christ, Christian salvation, the sanctity of the Bible, and even in God himself.

Lincoln even once declared Jesus a "bastard" while asserting that the Bible's miracles went against the laws of Nature. In fact, our liberal sixteenth president, who often criticized fellow politicians for mixing theology and politics, and who enjoyed arguing against the Bible in public, much preferred reading the works of atheists, like Thomas Paine, Count Volney (Constantin François de Chasseboeuf), and Voltaire, over the works of religionists.

Lincoln himself authored an essay demonstrating that, far from being inspired, the Bible was actually "uninspired" and historically inaccurate, and in Illinois in the mid 1830s, he wrote "a little book on infidelity." Lincoln was saved from eternal disgrace by one Samuel Hill, his employer at the time, who—knowing it would certainly ruin the author's future—ripped the manuscript from young Abe's hands and hurled it into a burning stove. If this book had survived, we can be sure that Lincoln would not be worshiped as the Christ-like, canonized figure he is today!

John T. Stuart, an acquaintance of Lincoln, wrote:

> I knew Mr. Lincoln when he first came here, and for years afterwards. He was an avowed and open infidel, sometimes bordered on atheism. I have often heard Lincoln and one W. D. Herndon, who was a freethinker, talk over this subject. Lincoln went further against Christian beliefs and doctrines and principles than any man I ever heard: he shocked me. I don't remember the exact line of his argument: suppose it was against the inherent defects, so called, of the Bible, and on grounds of reason. Lincoln always denied that Jesus was the Christ of God,—denied that Jesus was the Son of God, as understood and maintained by the Christian Church. The Rev. Dr. Smith, who wrote a letter, tried to convert Lincoln from infidelity so late as 1858, and couldn't do it.

Leftist Lincoln, the man who wanted to be all things to all people, did not like being accused of atheism, or "infidelity," as he called it, and he fought earnestly against the charge, particularly in the early part of his political career when it was most obvious and most well-known. When the accusation began appearing regularly in the newspapers, Lincoln exploded, firing off refutations, none of them in the least convincing.

As "a majority" of Lincoln's associates said they could prove he was an "infidel," few believed such defenses, particularly when his own associates and admirers contradicted him on the issue. One of these was his close friend Ward Hill Lamon, who wrote:

> Mr. Lincoln was never a member of any church, nor did he believe in the inspiration of the Scriptures in the sense understood by evangelical Christians. . . . Overwhelming testimony out of many mouths, and none stronger than out of his own, place these facts beyond controversy. . . . When he went to church at all, he went to mock, and came away to mimic.

Lincoln's own wife, Mary (Todd) Lincoln, who admitted that her husband had never committed himself to any conventional faith, said the following of his "religiosity":

> Mr. Lincoln had no hope and no faith in the usual acceptance of those words.

Lincoln's own remarks have condemned him for all time as an

atheist, or at the very least, a non-believing skeptic and agnostic. "I am not a Christian," he once told Newton Bateman, the Superintendent of Public Instruction for the state of Illinois. On another occasion, when Lincoln was considering fighting a duel with James A. Shields, his friends intervened saying that such violence was against the Bible and the teachings of Jesus. Lincoln snapped back: "The Bible is not my book, nor Christianity my profession."

As late as 1862, despite his promise to be more discreet about his atheism, Lincoln was still denouncing religion, and in particular Christianity. That year Judge John A. Wakefield had written Lincoln, inquiring as to whether he had finally accepted Christianity yet, to which the Yankee president replied:

> My earlier views of the unsoundness of the Christian scheme of salvation and the human origin of the scriptures have become clearer and stronger with advancing years and I see no reason for thinking I shall ever change them.

Around the same time, *Manford's Magazine* quoted Lincoln as saying:

> It will not do to investigate the subject of religion too closely, as it is apt to lead to Infidelity [i.e., atheism].

Religiosity has long been one of the major differences between South and North. Nowhere is this more apparent than in the political leaders of both sections. President Jefferson Davis, for example, proclaimed far more days of fasting and prayer than Lincoln, and while the U.S. Constitution is curiously lacking the word "God," the C.S. Constitution not only mentions him, but refers to him as "Almighty God."

Widely known as an "open scoffer of Christianity," Lincoln—the man who bragged that he had once written "a little book on infidelity," called Jesus a bastard, and belonged to no church—admitted that he embraced an atheistic concept called the "Doctrine of Necessity," in which according to Lincoln, "the human mind is impelled to action, or held at rest by some power, over which the mind itself has no control . . ." No definition of atheism has ever been more aptly or concisely expressed.[116]

FACT 92

THE NORTH DOESN'T WANT YOU TO KNOW THAT LINCOLN WAS A LIFELONG ADVOCATE OF BLACK DEPORTATION

From the earliest known records we find Lincoln supporting the idea of what was then known as "black colonization," the racist plan to deport all people of African descent to colonies in foreign countries, such as Liberia. The pro-North movement would rather you not know this. But even if you do, they would like you to believe that Lincoln rejected this idea before he became president.

As I have thoroughly covered this aspect of Lincoln's life in my other books, we will merely touch on it here. First, let us examine the Yankee claim that Lincoln stopped endorsing black colonization before he became president.

What historians call the Emancipation Proclamation was actually the final version of a document that underwent several minor and major revisions in draft form. As such, it would be more accurate to call the last one, issued January 1, 1863, the Final Emancipation Proclamation.

"I cannot make it better known than it already is, that I strongly favor colonization." U.S. President Abraham Lincoln, December 1, 1862, from his Second Annual Message to Congress.

The document that is of most interest to us in regards to this particular Northern myth, however, is known as the Preliminary Emancipation Proclamation, and what an interesting article it is. If only it was studied as closely as the Final Emancipation Proclamation, our sixteenth chief executive would never have been wrongly apotheosized as the "Great Emancipator"!

The Preliminary Emancipation Proclamation, which Lincoln said he "fixed up a little" over the previous weekend, then read to his cabinet on September 22, 1862—just four months before issuing the Final Emancipation Proclamation—contained the following remarkable statement:

> it is my purpose . . . to again recommend . . . that the effort to colonize [that is, deport] persons of African descent with their consent upon this continent or elsewhere . . . will be continued.

Why did this sensational clause, directed at the U.S. Congress, not make it into the Final Emancipation Proclamation? Against his wishes Lincoln's own cabinet members talked him out of including it because it might further alienate abolitionists, a group that was already bitterly disappointed with Lincoln's refusal to abolish slavery after being in the White House for over two years. Lincoln would need their votes in his upcoming bid for reelection in 1864. Promising to deport newly freed blacks out of the country was hardly the way to win the hearts, minds, and votes of the vociferous antislavery crowd. And so the item on black colonization, one of Lincoln's most ardent lifelong aspirations, was struck from the Final Emancipation Proclamation.

Thus this version, the only one known by the public today, is *not* the Emancipation Proclamation Lincoln wanted. It was the one forced on him by his cabinet and by political expediency.

But this did nothing to slow down his personal campaign to expel all African-Americans from the country. Indeed, shortly thereafter, just one month before issuing the Final Emancipation Proclamation, he reemphasized his position on the issue, lest anyone should forget. In his Second Annual Message to Congress on December 1, 1862, Lincoln stated unambiguously:

> I cannot make it better known than it already is, that I strongly favor colonization.

In this same speech he once again asks Congress to set aside funding for black deportation, even suggesting that it be added as an amendment to the Constitution in order to expedite it. According to Lincoln:

Congress may appropriate money and otherwise provide for colonizing free colored persons, with their own consent, at any place or places without the United States.

While Congress continued to allocate money for Lincoln's bizarre deportation scheme, by this time few politicians besides the president actually believed it was feasible.

When it came to the Northern populace, however, Lincoln was far from being alone in his desire to rid America of blacks. At the time, all across the North, white racism was deeply entrenched, far more so than in the much more racially tolerant South. Even Thaddeus Stevens, one of the North's most infamous and fervent abolitionists, had founded a colonization society devoted to freeing and deporting blacks.

Why were Lincoln and thousands of other white Northerners so keen to "cleanse" the U.S. of African-Americans?

It was the common Yankee belief, even among most Northern abolitionists, that people of African descent were inferior to those of European descent, inferior in intellect, morality, psychology, emotionality, creativity, and physicality. They were a kind of "bridge," or even a separate species, between apes and man, many white Northerners staunchly maintained.

Southern icon Confederate General Nathan Bedford Forrest is widely criticized by the uninformed for being a "racist." But it was Forrest who, after the War, repeatedly called for *importing* blacks into the country. It was Lincoln who repeatedly called for *deporting* blacks out of the country. Yet it is Lincoln and not Forrest who anti-South advocates consider a "friend of the black man." The pro-North version of the Civil War simply does not stand up to the facts. Revisionist history never does.

Respected Yankee historian James Ford Rhodes, for instance, described slaves as "indolent and filthy," "stupid" and "duplicitous," with "brute-like countenances." Esteemed New York physician and Union officer Robert Wilson Shufeldt, who wrote a book called, *The Negro: A*

Menace to American Society, came to the anthropological conclusion that blacks were an inferior race whose presence could only degrade the European-American community. As such, like Lincoln, Shufeldt spent much of his life developing ideas and methods by which to rid the United States of its African population. By way of deportation and colonization, wrote the Cornell University alumnus,

> we have it in our power to render the negro race extinct in the United States in very short order.

In Massachusetts blacks were widely regarded as a cross between a juvenile, a lunatic, and a "retard." Other Northerners were even less charitable. Famed Harvard scientist Louis Agassiz declared that "the negro race groped in barbarism and never originated a regular organization among themselves." Agassiz, like his English associate Charles Darwin (who originated the idea of natural selection, or "survival of the fittest"), believed that blacks were so evolutionarily feeble that once freed from slavery they would eventually "die out" in the U.S.

Thus no Northerners blinked, except a few authentic abolitionists, when on September 16, 1858, Lincoln made the following remarks during a senatorial debate with rival Stephen A. Douglas at Columbus, Ohio:

> . . . this is the true complexion of all I have ever said in regard to the institution of slavery and the black race. This is the whole of it, and anything that argues me into his idea of perfect social and political equality with the negro is but a specious and fantastic arrangement of words, by which a man can prove a horse-chestnut to be a chestnut horse. I will say here, while upon this subject, that I have no purpose either directly or indirectly to interfere with the institution of slavery in the States where it exists. I believe I have no lawful right to do so, and I have no inclination to do so. I have no purpose to introduce political and social equality between the white and the black races. There is a physical difference between the two which, in my judgment, will probably forever forbid their living together upon the footing of perfect equality, and inasmuch as it becomes a necessity that there must be a difference, I, as well as Judge Douglas, am in favor of the race to which I belong having the superior position. I have never said anything to the contrary .
> . . I agree with Judge Douglas, he [the black man] is not my equal

in many respects—certainly not in color, perhaps not in moral or intellectual endowments.

Lincoln preferred the idea of living in a black-free America, and his own words prove it.

Lincoln showing his cabinet the *Final* Emancipation Proclamation. At a previous meeting they had discussed the president's September 22, 1862, *Preliminary* Emancipation Proclamation, at which time they talked him into removing his infamous black colonization clause because it would offend abolitionists in his party. The redacted material included Lincoln's request of Congress that it apportion funds for his black colonization plan, which would deport freed slaves to foreign lands. The secretly deleted clause read: "It is my purpose . . . to again recommend . . . that the effort to colonize persons of African descent with their consent upon this continent or elsewhere . . . will be continued." Thus, the Final Emancipation Proclamation—*the only one known to the public*—is not the document Lincoln had originally wanted. It was the one that was forced on him by political expediency.

The motivating idea behind black deportation was that the freed negro "should be sent where he would never provoke friction with the whites," with Africa being "considered the most desirable place for the realization of this object." In 1819 the Board of Managers of the American Colonization Society issued a statement declaring that their goal was "the happiness of the free people of colour and the reduction of the number of slaves in America." The actual charter of the ACS states that its object is to promote and execute a plan for colonizing, with their consent, the free people of color residing in our country, either in Africa, or such other places as Congress shall deem expedient.

ACS supporter Samuel J. Mills of Connecticut put it this way: "We must save the negroes [through deportation], or the negroes will ruin us," a sentiment then widely held across Yankeedom.

Contrary to Yankee myth, Lincoln not only continued his campaign to free the U.S. of its black citizens throughout his entire presidency, he never abandoned the weird obsession. In fact, he lobbied feverishly for colonization right up to the day he died, two years after issuing the Emancipation Proclamation, as Yankee General Benjamin "the Beast" Butler attests. According to Butler, in April 1865, just days before Lincoln was assassinated by Northerner John Wilkes Booth, the president called the general to the White House to discuss the practicalities of black expatriation. Of the meeting Butler writes:

> A conversation was held between us after the negotiations had failed at Hampton Roads [February 3, 1865], and in the course of the conversation he [Lincoln] said to me: —
>
> 'But what shall we do with the negroes after they are free? I can hardly believe that the South and North can live in peace, unless we can get rid of the negroes. Certainly they cannot if we don't get rid of the negroes whom we have armed and disciplined and who have fought with us, to the amount, I believe of some one hundred and fifty thousand men. I believe that it would be better to export them all to some fertile country with a good climate, which they could have to themselves.
>
> 'You have been a staunch friend of the race from the time you first advised me to enlist them at New Orleans. You have had a good deal of experience in moving bodies of men by water,—your movement up the James was a magnificent one. Now we shall have no use for our very large navy; what, then, are our difficulties in sending all the blacks away?'

Butler responded by discussing his own idea of how to "send all the blacks away." The solution was simple: settle a colony for them in the Isthmus of Darien (modern Panama). To this Lincoln agreed, replying: "There is meat in that, General Butler; there is meat in that."

In 1922 historian J. G. de Roulhac Hamilton put it like this:

Lincoln's belief in colonization of the negro as a practical solution of the question never faltered. It was a major policy of his during the war in connection with emancipation.

Of this distasteful aspect of Lincoln's political career, in 1919 Charles H. Wesley wrote:

> From the earliest period of his public life it is easily discernable that Abraham Lincoln was an ardent believer and supporter of the colonization idea. It was his plan not only to emancipate the Negro, but to colonize him in some foreign land. His views were presented not only to interested men of the white race, but to persons of color as well. As may have been expected, the plan for colonization failed, both because in principle such a plan would have been a great injustice to the newly emancipated race, and in practice it would have proved an impracticable and unsuccessful solution of the so-called race problem.

The American Colonization Society issued this one cent token in 1833 for use in its African colony Liberia. The back of the coin (shown here) displays the organization's name and founding year. The development of Liberia delighted President Lincoln, who was himself not only a devoted benefactor of the colony, but who was at one time an ACS official in Illinois. His ongoing efforts in the cause of black deportation prompted one of his party's liberal members, Massachusetts-born Samuel Clarke Pomeroy, to suggest naming a freedmen's colony in Latin American "Linconia."

Emancipation first. Colonization second. This was Lincoln's plan for blacks from the beginning to the very end of his life. Had he survived Booth's attack, there is no question that he would have done everything in his power to fulfill the second half of his program. Thus it was, in great part, Booth who finally freed American blacks, not Abraham Lincoln. For the stark reality is that African-Americans, whether enslaved or free, would have never been completely liberated while Lincoln was alive—and indeed they were not. Booth's bullet was the true "Great Emancipator."[117]

THIRTY-SIXTH ANNUAL REPORT

OF THE

AMERICAN COLONIZATION SOCIETY,

WITH THE PROCEEDINGS OF THE

BOARD OF DIRECTORS AND OF THE SOCIETY;

AND THE ADDRESSES

DELIVERED AT THE ANNUAL MEETING,

January 18, 1853.

WASHINGTON:
C. ALEXANDER, PRINTER.
F ST., NEAR NAVY DEPARTMENT.
1853.

The cover of the American Colonization Society's 36th Annual Report, dated January 18, 1853, Washington, D.C. It includes proceedings from the Board of Directors of the ACS. ACS member and leader Lincoln no doubt read this report with great interest.

FACT 93

THE NORTH DOESN'T WANT YOU TO KNOW THAT ABRAHAM LINCOLN WAS NOT THE "FRIEND OF BLACKS" OR THE "GREAT EMANCIPATOR"

According to not only his party members but his own words, U.S. President Abraham Lincoln stalled emancipation, blocked black civil rights, promoted American apartheid, and spent his entire adult life pushing for the deportation of blacks. Indeed, as we have seen, he was a lifelong supporter and onetime leader of the racist Yankee organization, the American Colonization Society, whose stated goal was to make America "white from coast to coast," by shipping out as many blacks as possible to foreign lands.

If the public knew the truth about Lincoln his image would be immediately removed from the U.S. penny, the Illinois license plate, and Mt. Rushmore.

In point of fact, Lincoln was a callous Leftist and a publicly avowed white racist, white supremacist, and white separatist whose plans for African-Americans included corralling them in their own all-black state and exiling the rest back "to their own native land," as he phrased it in a speech at Peoria, Illinois, on October 16, 1854.

Not only that, Lincoln's Emancipation Proclamation did not actually free a single slave. This was because his edict only liberated slaves in the Confederate States, a sovereign nation where he had no legal authority, while leaving slavery intact in the United States, where he had full legal authority. For these reasons alone—and there are many others—Lincoln cannot be considered either the "friend of the black man" or the "Great Emancipator."[118]

FACT 94

THE NORTH DOESN'T WANT YOU TO KNOW THAT IN 1862 LINCOLN ISSUED A HUMAN "BLOCKADE" TO PREVENT FREED SOUTHERN BLACK SLAVES FROM MIGRATING INTO THE NORTHERN STATES

It was the same Yankee bigotry possessed by Lincoln that prompted one of his loyal employees, David Davis, associate justice of the Supreme Court, to go to the president and complain that an "excess" of freed Southern slaves venturing into Illinois would jeopardize his chances in the upcoming 1864 election. Lincoln agreed, issuing what John Y. Simon referred to as a human "blockade," one meant to halt even the possibility of a "negro influx" northward.

From then on Southern blacks made refugees by Lincoln's War were restricted to camps set up in the South by Union officers, where they were forced to work cotton under armed guard. Few white Northerners, especially Lincoln, wanted to be "tied down and helpless, and run over like sheep," as he himself put it on September 16, 1859, by an advancing horde of Southern African-Americans.[119]

Lincoln's associate justice of the Supreme Court, David Davis. In 1862, after Davis complained to his boss that an "excess" of freed Southern blacks coming into Illinois could potentially jeopardize the 1864 election, Lincoln issued a human "blockade" to prevent any more African-Americans from entering the Prairie State. If this did not work, Lincoln believed, they could be deported and colonized in Africa—an idea he had referred to in a speech at Peoria, Illinois, on October 16, 1854. Or, he could simply corral them in an all-black state (to be created by his administration)—a typically Northern idea he had announced publicly at the Lincoln-Douglas Debate on September 15, 1858.

FACT 95

THE NORTH DOESN'T WANT YOU TO KNOW THAT LINCOLN WAS NOT AGAINST SLAVERY, ONLY THE SPREAD OF SLAVERY

Lincoln always did what was most politically expedient at the moment, a trait for which he was roundly criticized, even by members of his own party and constituency. However, there was one topic on which he never wavered: slavery. But contrary to Yankee myth, Lincoln's number one goal when it came to slavery was never to totally eliminate it. It was merely to *limit* its growth, as he himself said on numerous occasions. He only later acquiesced to the idea of complete abolition due to pressure from party radicals and political self-interest.

On December 22, 1860, in a letter to Southerner and soon-to-be Confederate Vice President Alexander H. Stephens, Lincoln wrote: "You think slavery . . . ought to be extended; while we think it . . . ought to be restricted." "Honest Abe," for once being completely honest, ended his letter to Stephens with this sensational statement: This is the "only substantial difference between us."

Just a few months later, on March 4, 1861, he would repeat the same sentiment almost word for word in his First Inaugural Address:

> One section of our country believes slavery . . . ought to be extended, while the other believes it . . . ought not . . . be extended. This is the only substantial dispute.[120]

Thus, just prior to the War, Lincoln held that the only real difference between the South's view of slavery and the North's was that the former wanted to allow it to spread (mainly into the new Western Territories, eventually to become America's Western states), while the latter wanted to contain it where it already existed (that is, mainly in the South). No mention of emancipation or abolition. Just limitation.

Six years earlier, in his debate with Stephen A. Douglas on

October 16, 1854, at Peoria, Illinois, Lincoln outlined his reasons for wanting to restrict, not end, slavery:

> Whether slavery shall go into Nebraska, or other new Territories, is not a matter of exclusive concern to the people who may go there. The whole nation is interested that the best use shall be made of these Territories. We want them for homes of free white people. This they cannot be, to any considerable extent, if slavery shall be planted within them. Slave States are places for poor white people to remove from, not to remove to. New free States are the places for poor people to go to, and better their condition. For this use the nation needs these Territories.

Four years later, on October 15, 1858, at Alton, Illinois, in his seventh and final joint debate with Douglas, Lincoln reasserted his views on the matter, this time even more vigorously:

> Now, irrespective of the moral aspect of this question as to whether there is a right or wrong in enslaving a negro, I am still in favor of our new Territories being in such a condition that white men may find a home—may find some spot where they can better their condition—where they can settle upon new soil, and better their condition in life. I am in favor of this not merely (I must say it here as I have elsewhere) for our own people [that is, whites] who are born amongst us, but as an outlet for free white people everywhere, the world over—in which Hans, and Baptiste, and Patrick, and all other men from all the world, may find new homes and better their condition in life.

As he declared in a speech on June 26, 1857, the deportation of blacks was the only way to prevent whites from having to live in close association with them. But,

> as an immediate separation is impossible the next best thing is to keep them apart where they are not already together.

Thus, even if his racist colonization plan did not work out, he knew of other ways of "keeping whites and blacks apart where they are not already together."

Limiting the spread of slavery into the North was important to Lincoln and other Yankee racists for a number of reasons, though there was one that stood out above all the others. By forcing slavery to stay in the South they believed that this would also serve as an ideal method of "race control": keeping blacks in bondage in Dixie meant that Northerners need not worry about a "flood of darkies" coming over the Mason-Dixon Line any time soon, with whites "tied down and helpless, and run over like sheep," as Lincoln bluntly put it. With slavery confined to the South, Yanks could continue to promote antislavery views without fear of having to actually deal with the "unthinkable horror" of how to handle 3.5 million newly freed, hungry, homeless, and jobless blacks, many of them illiterate, armed, confused, and angry.

This is why for Lincoln the issue was never about permanent and total emancipation. Rather it was about containing the spread of slavery so that bigoted whites like himself would not have to intermingle with blacks. "If we do not let them [blacks] get together in the [Western] Territories," he said publicly on July 10, 1858, "they won't mix [with whites] there."

As U.S. President Woodrow Wilson writes, in Lincoln's mind it was not a question of slavery continuing in the South or anywhere else. It was a question of keeping it out of the newly developing Western Territories. On this issue in particular Lincoln had the "almost unanimous" support of the North, nearly all of whose inhabitants agreed with the president that the territories should remain "as white as New England." One of Lincoln's own senators, Lyman Trumbull, summed up the president's feelings on the matter perfectly when he referred to their political party as "the white man's party."[121]

President Lincoln revealed his *true* views on blacks and slavery countless times. On February 1, 1861, for example, he told his secretary of state, William H. Seward:

> As to fugitive slaves, . . . slave-trade among the slave States, and whatever springs of necessity from the fact that the institution is amongst us, I care but little . . .

Later, at the Hampton Roads Conference on February 3, 1865, Lincoln told Confederate diplomats that since the Emancipation Proclamation was a "war measure," it would end with the War. After that, for all he cared, the South would be free to continue slavery if it wished.[122]

FACT 96

THE NORTH DOESN'T WANT YOU TO KNOW THAT LINCOLN'S EMANCIPATION PROCLAMATION DID NOT FREE A SINGLE SLAVE, & WAS NOT INTENDED TO

It is well-known to educated Southerners today that the Final Emancipation Proclamation, issued January 1, 1863, only "freed" slaves in the South, and even then, only in specific areas of the South. Lincoln's edict purposefully excluded Tennessee, for example (the entire state had been under Yankee control since the fall of Nashville, February 25, 1862), all of the Border States, and numerous Northern-occupied parishes in Louisiana and several counties in Virginia.

The Final Emancipation Proclamation, in fact, was issued only in areas of the South not under Union control; that is, it only "freed" Southern slaves who had sided with the Confederacy. It did not ban slavery anywhere in the North, where thousands of Yankees still practiced it, including Union officers like General Ulysses S. Grant and his family. As Lincoln states in the proclamation itself, the entire North, as well as those Southern places that were exempted, "are for the present left precisely as if this proclamation were not issued." He could not have made the meaning of this sentence more clear: *slavery was to be allowed to continue in the U.S. (that is, the North) and in any areas of the C.S. (that is, the South) controlled by the U.S. (that is, by the Union armies).*

The question Southerners have been asking Northerners for the past century and a half is why, if Lincoln was so interested in black equality, did he only abolish slavery in the South where he had no jurisdiction but not in the North where he had full control?

The answer is obvious to most Southerners today, just as it was to a majority of them in 1863: the Emancipation Proclamation was nothing more than a clever political illusion, for he did not free slaves where he legally could (in the North and in the Border States), yet he sought to free them (in the South) where he had no legal right to do so.

If Northerners had asked themselves this same question at the time, they would have never created the myth of Lincoln the "Great Emancipator" to begin with!

In truth our sixteenth president did not issue the Emancipation Proclamation for the specific purpose of trying to establish black civil rights across the U.S. If that had indeed been his intention he would have also banned slavery in the North and in non-Union occupied areas of the South.

Being the penultimate politician, halfway through his war Lincoln decided that it would be politically expedient to shift the character of the conflict from "preserving the Union" to "abolishing slavery." Both were rank falsehoods, however, carefully calculated to procure Northern and abolitionist votes in the upcoming 1864 presidential election. Part of this devilish ruse was the issuance of the Final Emancipation Proclamation on January 1, 1863, which, revealingly, he publicly referred to not as a "civil rights measure," but as a "*war measure*"; not as a "civil rights emancipation," but as a "*military emancipation*." Thus according to Lincoln himself, the edict did not have a single thing to do with black equality or even true abolition.

Abraham Lincoln's Emancipation Proclamation was a sham, and an illegal and toothless one at that. The truth behind it was revealed by the Mephistophelian Union president himself when he called it a "military emancipation" and a "war measure."

Yet, what a dastardly brilliant idea it was. For no one could argue against emancipation—not even the most pro-South Northerners or pro-North Southerners—if Lincoln could prove that freeing the slaves was vital to winning the War. Assuming that he would reap untold benefits from this shift in the character of the conflict from a political basis to a moral one, it did not matter whether or not any Southern slaves were actually freed to not. And thus legally none were.[123]

FACT 97

THE NORTH DOESN'T WANT YOU TO KNOW THAT LINCOLN ONLY ISSUED THE EMANCIPATION PROCLAMATION FOR POLITICAL & MILITARY PURPOSES, NOT TO HELP AFRICAN-AMERICANS

Despite his cynical backroom conniving, President Lincoln did hope that his Emancipation Proclamation would yield results beyond merely garnering public support. But why did he wait nearly three years before issuing the document? If he was concerned about black civil rights, as pro-North advocates claim, why did he wait so long, only succumbing after years of pressure and harassment?[124]

The fact is that Lincoln issued the proclamation with five primary wishes in mind: 1) He hoped it would secure Europe's support. 2) He hoped it would instigate slave rebellions across the South. 3) He hoped to procure new troops to compensate for his drastically declining white soldiery. 4) He hoped to get new voters for the upcoming 1864 election. 5) He needed to free black slaves before he could deport them.

Unfortunately for him, all five reasons were utter failures, for he was widely known among Southern blacks as a white racist who detested the abolitionist movement; who delayed abolition for as long as possible; was a leader in the American Colonization Society; forced slaves to complete the construction of the Capitol dome in Washington, D.C.; implemented extreme racist military policies; used profits from Northern slavery to fund his War; referred to blacks as "niggers"; said he was willing to allow slavery to continue in perpetuity if the Southern states would come back into the Union; engaged in a lifelong campaign to deport all American blacks; as a lawyer defended slave owners in court; backed the proslavery Corwin Amendment to the Constitution in 1861; and continually blocked black enlistment, black suffrage, and black citizenship. All of this is why Frederick Douglass said that Lincoln's attitude toward blacks lacked "the genuine spark of humanity."[125]

FACT 98

THE NORTH DOESN'T WANT YOU TO KNOW THAT LINCOLN COMPARED FREED SLAVES TO WILD HOGS, DECLARING: "LET 'EM ROOT, PIG, OR PERISH!"

Lincoln had absolutely no formal plan for dealing with the millions of Southern slaves he intended to suddenly liberate in January 1863. If he truly cared about African-Americans, as we are asked to believe, this makes no sense whatsoever.

The reality is that he cared little for blacks, and he seldom tried to hide the fact. Once, when asked what was to become of emancipated blacks after they were "freed" by his Emancipation Proclamation, he likened them to wild hogs, and said: "Let 'em root, pig, or perish!"—and that is exactly what occurred, as our next entry shows.[126]

Lincoln's Emancipation Proclamation contained no plans for freed black slaves, no provisions for housing, food, clothing, employment, or healthcare. They were merely "turned loose" to fend for themselves or end up on so-called "government plantations" like this one, malodorous squatter camps where poverty, sickness, hunger, thievery, and prostitution reigned. In February 1865, when Confederate diplomats asked Lincoln what he planned to do with America's 4.5 million freed slaves (North and South), he likened them to hogs, and jokingly replied: "Let 'em root, pig, or perish!" The president may have thought this was humorous, but he was the only one who laughed.

THE NORTH IS STILL LYING ABOUT LINCOLN'S WAR

FACT 99

THE NORTH DOESN'T WANT YOU TO KNOW THAT LINCOLN'S EMANCIPATION PROCLAMATION KILLED OFF 25 PERCENT OF ALL SOUTHERN BLACKS, MAKING IT AN EPIC NATIONAL DISASTER

After the issuance of the Final Emancipation Proclamation on January 1, 1863, only three things happened immediately: Union recruitment plummeted, Union desertion skyrocketed, and the quality of life for blacks sank to an all time low, remaining far beneath even slavery levels for the next 100 years.

After the War, for instance, black life span dropped 10 percent, diets and health deteriorated, disease and sickness rates went up 20 percent, the number of skilled blacks declined, and the gap between white and black wages widened, trends that did not even begin to reverse until the onset of World War II, 75 years later, in 1939. At least one out of four "freed" blacks died in a number of Southern communities.

Lincoln's Emancipation Proclamation did not come close to accomplishing what he had hoped it would. Instead it instigated a host of social issues that plague us to this day. One of the more notorious of these left-wing legacies is the burdensome nanny state: an overly controlling, overly powerful, and overly interfering U.S. central government that seeks to infantilize its citizens by making them feel entitled to—as well as dependent on—the Fed.

Of life after January 1, 1863, Adeline Grey, a black South Carolina servant, wrote that when "liberation" came she could still vividly remember it, while slavery was but a dim memory. Why?

Because "life was much more difficult and painful after emancipation than before."

The "pain" of emancipation was due, in great part, to the fact that Lincoln never pushed through any kind of organized, gradual, or compensated emancipation plan, as nearly every other Western nation had done when it abolished slavery. His proclamation, for example, contained no plans for freed black slaves, no provisions for housing, food, clothing, employment, or healthcare.

Freed slaves were merely "turned loose" to fend for themselves; literally cast out into the streets with no education, no jobs, no shelter, no job training, no grants or loans. The more unfortunate ended up on so-called "government plantations," odiferous squatter camps that bred little but despair, disease, crime, starvation, and harlotry.

And Lincoln's promise to freedmen of "forty acres and a mule" was little more than a carrot on the end of a stick, used to lure blacks into a false sense of governmental protection after emancipation. After all, his so-called "black land giveaways" were never meant to be permanent, and what little of these were dispersed went primarily to wealthy white Northerners.

This ridiculous and misleading piece of pro-North propaganda portrays Lincoln as "The Great Emancipator." He was anything but. Not only did he delay abolition for as long as possible and block black advancement at every turn, he also supported the Corwin Amendment, campaigned to have all blacks deported, and refused to issue the Emancipation Proclamation until he was forced to by political expediency: he was running out of white soldiers *and* needed the abolitionist vote for his reelection in 1864. And still the unenlightened continue to call him "The Great Emancipator"! As Lincoln was the ultimate demagogue, a more appropriate title would be "The Great Impersonator," which is how I refer to him in the title of my book of the same name.

Under Lincoln's "root, pig, or perish" emancipation plan, blacks who as servants had lived quality lives equal to and often superior to many whites and free blacks, now found themselves living out in the open or in makeshift tents, begging for food and work. There was now less labor available to them under freedom than there had been under servitude, and thus the once booming Southern black economic system plunged.

Disease, homelessness, starvation, and beggary now became the lot of untold thousands of former black servants. Even many of those who managed to become sharecroppers eventually found themselves in a state of peonage (a debt that tied them to the land), living in crude filthy shacks, suffering from illiteracy, ill health, and malnutrition. All of this was a far cry from the excellent quality of life experienced by Southern blacks when they had lived as "slaves." By 1867, just four years after the Emancipation Proclamation was issued, 1 million, or 25 percent, of all Southern blacks had perished from starvation, neglect, infanticide, corruption, and disease.

Within months after it was issued it was already plain that Lincoln's Emancipation Proclamation was going to be a failure and a disaster of nationwide proportions, and he admitted as much when he called it "the greatest folly of my life." However, the true folly was that the North voted an unqualified, big government Liberal into the White House to begin with; one who himself stated that he was "not fit to be president." That these facts have for so long been concealed by the anti-South movement is surely a blight on the North's reputation, a travesty against the America people, and an insult to the countless thousands who gave their lives in Lincoln's War—both Confederate and Union. If there were no other reason for exposing The Great Yankee Coverup, this alone would suffice.

Due to how it was handled, the Emancipation Proclamation was truly a national disaster on an epic scale, as Lincoln himself admitted. It was "the greatest folly of my life," he later opined. And we in the South agree.[127]

This 19th-Century left-wing illustration ridiculously equates Liberal U.S. President Abraham Lincoln with Conservative U.S. President George Washington, inferring that "under providence," Washington "made" our country while Lincoln "saved" it, a preposterous myth still being promulgated by The Great Yankee Coverup. In 1869 Pennsylvania attorney and Episcopal preacher Henry Clay Dean, a Copperhead, noted the differences between the two men this way:

>Washington was modest, reticent, dignified. Lincoln was familiar, garrulous and clownish. Washington was wise, sincere and determined. Lincoln was cunning, treacherous and fickle. Washington refused presents, pay for his services, and emoluments for his sacrifices. Lincoln kept each member of his family as beggars for presents, silent partners in contracts, and grew wealthy from the spoils of office. Washington established constitutional liberty among men, upon the sure foundations of law. Lincoln tore up that very Constitution, and set up his arbitrary will instead. Washington was religiously careful in the selection of the ablest, purest men of the country to administer the government; choosing those who differed with him in opinion, for the good of the country. Lincoln selected the weakest, worst and most corrupt men of the country, because they agreed with him in opinion, and served him cheerfully as instruments of usurpation. Washington moulded chaos into order, stability and legitimate government. Lincoln dissolved the government, and left the country in anarchy. Washington received the spontaneous devotion of his countrymen through the press which he had made free, and the people who were secure in their liberty. Lincoln enforced the most extravagant adulation from his own hired presses, his officers who were plundering the country, and the pulpit bribed to chant his praises. Washington went to every part of the land, unattended by military array, except those crowds of old volunteers of liberty, who came to pay their respect to his person, and congratulate the country upon the success of constitutional government. Women, with woven garlands, met him wherever he went. Beautiful maidens and sweet little children, strewed his walks with flowers. From the day of the inauguration to the hour of his tragical death, Lincoln was never out of the reach of the sound of artillery; was surrounded by soldiers to guard his person; flatterers and courtiers to corrupt his heart; and female sycophants begging favors, dispensing praises, and making merry in his court.
>   After his term of office, Washington retired to his farm, to open the hospitable door of his mansion to his old confreres in arms, and entertain visitors who sought his company to learn more of manly liberty. In the strength of his mind and the vigor of a green old age, surrounded by friends who loved him, he surrendered his soul to God, to be mourned by his countrymen and honored by

mankind. Lincoln closed his life as stated above.

There was a singular resemblance between the Roman Emperor Claudius Nero, and Abraham Lincoln. In early life, Nero was remarkable for his jovial habit of illustration. Lincoln's whole field of logic, illustration, ridicule and satire, was anecdote and stories. Nero proposed many reforms under Seneca and Burrhus, and grew in popularity among the people, until he was accounted a god. Lincoln commenced his administration as a benevolent reformer, under the auspices of all the reformers of the country. Nero's subjects rebelled against his usurpation. Lincoln's subjects anticipated his usurpation. Such rulers always create rebellions and excite resistance.

Nero played the drama of the destruction of Troy, during the seven days' burning of Rome. Lincoln attended balls and engaged in festivities during the five years' conflagration of the country, and the wanton, bloody slaughter of his countrymen; and had vile songs sung among his dying armies. Nero rebuilt Rome at his own expense, by extortion and robbery, and the tyrant was liberal to the sufferers. In this Nero excelled Lincoln, who repaired no damages of burning cities.

Nero threw prisoners to wild beasts. Lincoln kept prisoners confined in cold prisons, where their limbs were frozen; in filthy prisons where they were eaten up with vermin; starved them until they died of scurvy and other loathesome diseases, after months of terror, torture and cruelty. Nero put Christians to death under false pretence, to gratify the worshippers of the Pantheon. Lincoln corrupted one part of the Church to engage in warfare with the other part, and burned twelve hundred houses of worship; mutilated grave-yards; and left whole cities, churches and all in ashes; dragged ministers from their knees in the very act of worship; tied them up by their thumbs; had their daughters stripped naked by negro soldiers, under the command of white officers.

Suetonius, under Nero, butchered eighty thousand Britons, defended by Queen Boadicea. His officers flogged Boadicea and ravished her daughters; and lost thousands of Romans in the attempt to subdue the Britons, who were defending their homes, altars and grave-yards. Lincoln let loose [John B.] Turchin to ravish the women of Athens, Alabama; [Nathaniel P.] Banks and [Benjamin F.] Butler to rob New Orleans; [Philip] Sheridan to burn up Virginia; [William T.] Sherman to ravage the South with desolating fires; Payne and [Stephen G.] Burbridge to murder in Kentucky; [John] McNeil, [William] Strachan and the vagabond thieves, to murder, rob and destroy Missouri, until one million of his murdered countrymen butchered each other by his command.

Every department of Nero's government was signalized by licentiousness and debauchery, nameless and loathsome. Lincoln's court was the resort of debauchees; the Treasury Department was a harem; the public officers were one great unrestrained multitude who yielded to the coarsest appetites of nature, stimulated by strong drinks and inflamed by the indulgence of every other vice. In this did Nero, to his credit, differ from Lincoln. The generals of Nero respected the works of arts, the paintings, poems and manuscripts of the learned, and the discoveries of genius.

Upon the other hand, Lincoln destroyed everything that indicated superior civilization. In one instance, a [Union] general officer of scientific pretension, arrayed his daughter in the stolen garments of the wife of Clement C. Clay, an old Senator of Alabama. During the invasion of Huntsville, [Alabama] Mr. Clay's house was robbed of its jewelry, the heir-looms of three generations, taken against the tearful prayers of his black servant. The exquisitely beautiful statue of his dead babe, was ground to powder before his eyes. An appeal to Lincoln's men, that any object was of scientific value, only hastened its destruction; his wars were directed against civilization.

Nero fled before the judgment of the Senate, and died by his own hand. Lincoln could not have survived his crimes, so unrelenting is the retributive justice of God.[128] — Henry Clay Dean

The End of the Great Yankee Coverup!

NOTES

FOOTNOTING EVERY STATEMENT IN THIS BOOK WOULD ADD DOZENS OF PAGES. TO KEEP THE LENGTH DOWN, AS WELL AS FOR EASE OF USE, I HAVE PLACED (IN MOST CASES) A SINGLE ENDNOTE AT THE END OF EACH FACT ENTRY, DIRECTING THE READER TO MY EARLIER WORKS WHERE THE THOUSANDS OF ORIGINAL SOURCES CAN BE FOUND.

1. See Jones, TDMV, pp. 144, 200-201, 273.
2. See Seabrook, TAHSR, passim. See also, Pollard, LC, p. 178; Franklin, pp. 101, 111, 130, 149; Nicolay and Hay, ALCW, Vol. 1, p. 627.
3. See e.g., Seabrook, TQJD, pp. 30, 38, 76.
4. Seabrook, EYWTATCWIW, p. 13.
5. For the truth about the KKK, see Seabrook, EYWTATCWIW, pp. 193-195.
6. Seabrook, C101, pp. 23, 24, 31-38.
7. Seabrook, C101, pp. 39-40.
8. Seabrook, C101, pp. 41-42.
9. Seabrook, C101, p. 44.
10. Seabrook, C101, pp. 45-51.
11. Seabrook, EYWTATCWIW, pp. 52-57.
12. Seabrook, C101, pp. 60-61.
13. Seabrook, C101, pp. 54-55.
14. Seabrook, C101, p. 59.
15. Seabrook, C101, p. 71.
16. Seabrook, C101, pp. 75-76.
17. Seabrook, C101, p. 103.
18. Seabrook, EYWTAASIW, pp. 395-397.
19. Seabrook, EYWTATCWIW, pp. 33-37.
20. Seabrook, EYWTATCWIW, pp. 23-25.
21. Seabrook, S101, pp. 74-79.
22. Seabrook, C101, p. 89.
23. Seabrook, AL, pp. 47-48.
24. Seabrook, S101, pp. 80-81.
25. Seabrook, C101, p. 90.
26. For more on this topic see Seabrook, TQJD, passim; Seabrook, TAHSR, passim; Seabrook, TQAHS, passim.
27. Confederate Veteran, September 1900, Vol. 8, No. 9, p. 397. Emphasis added.
28. Knight, pp. 14, 138, 218. Emphasis added.
29. Seabrook, EYWTAASIW, p. 709. Emphasis added.
30. For more on the many comparisons between Lincoln and Hitler, see Seabrook, CFF, passim.
31. Seabrook, EYWTATCWIW, pp. 31-32.
32. Seabrook, S101, p. 83.
33. Seabrook, EYWTAASIW, pp. 784-785.
34. Seabrook, S101, p. 84.
35. Seabrook, EYWTATCWIW, pp. 171-173.
36. Seabrook, EYWTATCWIW, p. 29.
37. Seabrook, EYWTATCWIW, pp. 29-30.
38. Seabrook, EYWTATCWIW, p. 25.
39. Seabrook, EYWTATCWIW, p. 32.
40. Seabrook, EYWTATCWIW, p. 187.
41. See my book *A Rebel Born: A Defense of Nathan Bedford Forrest*.
42. Seabrook, EYWTATCWIW, pp. 112-113.

43. Seabrook, EYWTATCWIW, pp. 47-51.
44. Seabrook, AL, pp. 76-77.
45. Seabrook, EYWTAASIW, p. 220.
46. Seabrook, EYWTAASIW, pp. 61-68.
47. Seabrook, S101, pp. 27-28.
48. Seabrook, S101, p. 29.
49. Seabrook, EYWTAASIW, pp. 182-183.
50. Seabrook, EYWTAASIW, pp. 549-551, 570-571.
51. Seabrook, EYWTAASIW, pp. 48, 244.
52. Seabrook, S101, p. 11.
53. For more on the true history of prostitution, see my book *Aphrodite's Trade*.
54. Seabrook, S101, p. 13.
55. Seabrook, EYWTATCWIW, pp. 73-74.
56. Seabrook, EYWTAASIW, pp. 62-64.
57. Seabrook, EYWTAASIW, p. 65.
58. Seabrook, EYWTAASIW, p. 279.
59. Seabrook, EYWTAASIW, pp. 87-88, 94-96.
60. Seabrook, EYWTAASIW, pp. 125-153.
61. Seabrook, EYWTAASIW, pp. 155-163.
62. Seabrook, EYWTAASIW, pp. 62-96, 155-163.
63. Seabrook, EYWTAASIW, pp. 108-114.
64. Seabrook, EYWTAASIW, pp. 215-216.
65. Seabrook, EYWTAASIW, pp. 172, 216-219.
66. Seabrook, EYWTAASIW, pp. 220-222, 441.
67. Seabrook, EYWTAASIW, p. 420.
68. Seabrook, EYWTAASIW, pp. 273, 426.
69. Seabrook, EYWTAASIW, pp. 270, 425-426.
70. Seabrook, EYWTAASIW, pp. 459-460.
71. Lincoln called his "Emancipation Proclamation" exactly what it was: not a civil rights emancipation, but a "military emancipation." In other words, its true purpose was to "liberate" black servants, not so they could be free, but so the liberal Yankee president could use them in his armies. See e.g., Seabrook, L, p. 647.
72. Seabrook, EYWTAASIW, pp. 270, 329-330.
73. Seabrook, EYWTAASIW, pp. 304-316, 321-322, 442, 668, 674, 796, 823.
74. Seabrook, EYWTAASIW, pp. 583-584, 586.
75. Seabrook, EYWTAASIW, pp. 647-648.
76. Seabrook, EYWTAASIW, pp. 208, 252-254.
77. Seabrook, EYWTAASIW, pp. 647-648.
78. Seabrook, EYWTAASIW, pp. 654-655.
79. Seabrook, EYWTAASIW, pp. 106, 108, 251-252.
80. Seabrook, EYWTAASIW, pp. 242-243.
81. Seabrook, EYWTAASIW, pp. 599, 612.
82. Seabrook, EYWTAASIW, pp. 236-239, 745-754.
83. See my six works on Forrest: 1) *A Rebel Born: A Defense of Nathan Bedford Forrest - Confederate General, American Legend*; 2) *Nathan Bedford Forrest: Southern Hero, American Patriot - Honoring a Confederate Icon and the Old South*; 3) *The Quotable Nathan Bedford Forrest: Selections From the Writings and Speeches of the Confederacy's Most Brilliant Cavalryman*; 4) *Give 'Em Hell Boys! The Complete Military Correspondence of Nathan Bedford Forrest*; 5) *Forrest! 99 Reasons to Love Nathan Bedford Forrest*; 6) *Saddle, Sword, and Gun: A Biography of Nathan Bedford Forrest For Teens*.
84. See my two books on Lee: 1) *The Quotable Robert E. Lee: Selections From the Writings and Speeches of the South's Most Beloved Civil War General*; 2) *The Old Rebel: Robert E. Lee As He Was Seen By His Contemporaries*.
85. Seabrook, EYWTAASIW, pp. 220, 571-572, 596, 622.
86. See Seabrook, C101, passim.
87. Seabrook, EYWTAASIW, p. 736.
88. Seabrook, EYWTAASIW, pp. 230-231, 541, 549, 571.

89. Seabrook, EYWTATCWIW, pp. 85-86.
90. Seabrook, EYWTAASIW, pp. 244-249.
91. Seabrook, EYWTAASIW, pp. 335-336.
92. See my two books on Lee: 1) *The Quotable Robert E. Lee: Selections From the Writings and Speeches of the South's Most Beloved Civil War General*; 2) *The Old Rebel: Robert E. Lee As He Was Seen By His Contemporaries*.
93. Seabrook, EYWTAASIW, pp. 799-802.
94. Seabrook, EYWTAASIW, pp. 524, 860-863.
95. Seabrook, C101, p. 102.
96. Seabrook, EYWTAASIW, p. 273.
97. For more on Stephens and his genuine attitude toward African-Americans, see Seabrook, TAHSR, passim; and Seabrook, TQAHS, passim.
98. Seabrook, S101, p. 67.
99. Seabrook, EYWTAASIW, pp. 260-264.
100. Seabrook, EYWTAASIW, pp. 441-443.
101. Seabrook, C101, p. 98.
102. Seabrook, C101, p. 99.
103. Seabrook, C101, p. 100.
104. Seabrook, EYWTAASIW, p. 280.
105. Seabrook, EYWTAASIW, pp. 240-242.
106. Seabrook, EYWTAASIW, pp. 96-108.
107. Seabrook, EYWTAASIW, pp. 174-175.
108. Seabrook, EYWTAASIW, pp. 689-690.
109. Seabrook, EYWTAASIW, pp. 164-165.
110. Seabrook, AL, p. 258; Seabrook, EYWTATCWIW, p. 112.
111. Seabrook, EYWTATCWIW, pp. 109-110.
112. Seabrook, EYWTATCWIW, p. 110.
113. Seabrook, C101, p. 100.
114. Seabrook, EYWTATCWIW, pp. 113-114.
115. Seabrook, EYWTATCWIW, pp. 45-46.
116. Seabrook, AL, pp. 495-504.
117. See Seabrook, EYWTAASIW, pp. 734-779.
118. See Seabrook, AL, passim; Seabrook, TGI, passim; Seabrook, TUAL, passim; Seabrook, L, passim.
119. Seabrook, EYWTAASIW, p. 677.
120. Liberal Lincoln was promoting anti-South Yankee propaganda here. The Conservative South never once demanded that "slavery ought to be extended." She only asked that individuals be given the choice as to whether or not they practiced slavery in the new Western Territories. After all, the institution was still legal under the Constitution at the time. As always, the South's main interest was the preservation of individual and states' rights, not the preservation of slavery.
121. Seabrook, EYWTAASIW, pp. 772-776.
122. Seabrook, AL, pp. 372-373.
123. Seabrook, EYWTAASIW, pp. 609, 611, 686-688, 694.
124. Lincoln's procrastination toward issuing the Emancipation Proclamation earned him numerous unflattering titles from fellow Republicans, such as "the tortoise president" and "the slow coach at Washington." Seabrook, EYWTAASIW, p. 696.
125. Seabrook, EYWTAASIW, pp. 686-694, 732, 764.
126. Seabrook, EYWTAASIW, pp. 718-719.
127. Seabrook, EYWTAASIW, pp. 722-726, 810.
128. Seabrook, AL, pp. 571-573.

BIBLIOGRAPHY

Franklin, John Hope. *Reconstruction After the Civil War.* Chicago, IL: University of Chicago Press, 1961.
Jones, John William. *The Davis Memorial Volume; or Our Dead President and the World's Tribute to His Memory.* Richmond, VA: B. F. Johnson, 1889.
Knight, Lucian Lamar. *Memorials of Dixie-Land: Orations, Essays, Sketches and Poems on Topics Historical, Commemorative, Literary and Patriotic.* Atlanta, GA: self-published, 1919.
Nicolay, John George, and John Hay (eds.). *Abraham Lincoln: Complete Works.* 12 vols. New York, NY: The Century Co., 1907.
Pollard, Edward Alfred. *The Lost Cause.* New York, NY: E. B. Treat and Co., 1867.
Seabrook, Lochlainn. *Aphrodite's Trade: The Hidden History of Prostitution Unveiled.* 1993. Franklin, TN: Sea Raven Press, 2011 ed.
——. *Abraham Lincoln: The Southern View.* 2007. Franklin, TN: Sea Raven Press, 2013 ed.
——. *Nathan Bedford Forrest: Southern Hero, American Patriot: Honoring a Confederate Hero and the Old South.* 2007. Franklin, TN: Sea Raven Press, 2010 ed.
——. *A Rebel Born: A Defense of Nathan Bedford Forrest.* 2010. Franklin, TN: Sea Raven Press, 2011 ed.
——. *Everything You Were Taught About the Civil War is Wrong, Ask a Southerner!* 2010. Franklin, TN: Sea Raven Press, revised 2014 ed.
——. *The Quotable Jefferson Davis: Selections From the Writings and Speeches of the Confederacy's First President.* Franklin, TN: Sea Raven Press, 2011.
——. *Lincolnology: The Real Abraham Lincoln Revealed In His Own Words.* Franklin, TN: Sea Raven Press, 2011.
——. *The Unquotable Abraham Lincoln: The President's Quotes They Don't Want You To Know!* Franklin, TN: Sea Raven Press, 2011.
——. *The Quotable Robert E. Lee: Selections From the Writings and Speeches of the South's Most Beloved Civil War General.* 2011. Franklin, TN: Sea Raven Press, 2014 ed.
——. *The Constitution of the Confederate States of America Explained: A Clause-by-Clause Study of the South's Magna Carta.* Franklin, TN: Sea Raven Press, 2012.
——. *The Old Rebel: Robert E. Lee As He Was Seen By His Contemporaries.* Franklin, TN: Sea Raven Press, 2012.
——. *The Quotable Stonewall Jackson: Selections From the Writings and Speeches of the South's Most Famous General.* Franklin, TN: Sea Raven Press, 2012.
——. *Give 'Em Hell Boys! The Complete Military Correspondence of Nathan Bedford Forrest.* Franklin, TN: Sea Raven Press, 2012 Sesquicentennial Civil War Edition.
——. *Forrest! 99 Reasons to Love Nathan Bedford Forrest.* Franklin, TN: Sea Raven Press, 2012 Sesquicentennial Civil War Edition.
——. *The Quotable Nathan Bedford Forrest: Selections From the Writings and Speeches of the Confederacy's Most Brilliant Cavalryman.* Franklin, TN: Sea Raven Press, 2012 Sesquicentennial Civil War Edition.
——. *The Great Impersonator: 99 Reasons to Dislike Abraham Lincoln.* Franklin, TN: Sea Raven Press, 2012.
——. *Saddle, Sword, and Gun: A Biography of Nathan Bedford Forrest For Teens.* Franklin, TN: Sea Raven Press, 2013 Sesquicentennial Civil War Edition.
——. *The Alexander H. Stephens Reader: Excerpts From the Works of a Confederate Founding Father.* Franklin, TN: Sea Raven Press, 2013.
——. *The Quotable Alexander H. Stephens: Selections From the Writings and Speeches of the Confederacy's First Vice President.* Franklin, TN: Sea Raven Press, 2013.
——. *The Articles of Confederation Explained: A Clause-by-Clause Study of America's First Constitution.* Franklin, TN: Sea Raven Press, 2014.
——. *Give This Book to a Yankee: A Southern Guide to the Civil War For Northerners.* Franklin, TN: Sea Raven Press, 2014.
——. *Everything You Were Taught About American Slavery War is Wrong, Ask a Southerner!* Franklin, TN: Sea Raven Press, 2015.
——. *Confederacy 101: Amazing Facts You Never Knew About America's Oldest Political Tradition.* Franklin, TN: Sea Raven Press, 2015.
——. *Slavery 101: Amazing Facts You Never Knew About America's "Peculiar Institution".* Franklin, TN: Sea Raven Press, 2015.
——. *Confederate Blood and Treasure: An Interview With Lochlainn Seabrook.* Franklin, TN: Sea Raven Press, 2015.
——. *Confederate Flag Facts: What Every American Should Know About Dixie's Southern Cross.* Franklin, TN: Sea Raven Press, 2015.

INDEX

Adams, John, 13, 27, 130
Adams, John Q., 36
Adams, Samuel, 27
Adams, Shelby L., 207
Agassiz, Louis, 176
Alcott, Louisa M., 50
Allan, William T., 94
Anderson, Loni, 207
Anderson, Robert, 52
Andrew, Saint, 48
Andrews, Ethan A., 93
Arthur, King, 206
Astor, John J., 112
Atkins, Chet, 207
Baldwin, Henry, 148
Barksdale, Ethelbert, 141
Bateman, Newton, 172
Beauregard, Pierre G. T., 47, 51, 141, 207
Beecher, Henry W., 26
Bellamy, Francis, 60
Benjamin, Judah P., 152
Benton, Thomas H., 27
Bernstein, Leonard, 207
Birney, James G., 94
Blackburn, Gideon, 94
Blair, Montgomery, 51
Bolling, Edith, 207
Boone, Daniel, 207
Boone, Pat, 207
Booth, John Wilkes, 178, 179
Boudinot, Elias, 29
Bouiness, John, 154
Bourne, George, 94, 105

Brackett, Jeffrey R., 109
Breckinridge, John C., 207
Brooke, Edward W., 207
Brooks, Preston S., 207
Brown, John, 50
Buchanan, Patrick J., 207
Buckingham, James S., 87
Buffum, Arnold, 155
Buford, Abraham, 207
Bunyan, John, 118
Burbridge, Stephen G., 194
Burgess, Dyer, 94
Burrhus, 194
Butler, Andrew P., 207
Butler, Benjamin F., 178, 194
Butler, James B., 208
Calhoun, John C., 97
Cameron, Simon, 52
Campbell, Joseph, 206
Carson, Martha, 207
Carter, Theodrick "Tod", 207
Cash, Johnny, 207
Cass, Lewis, 28
Caudill, Benjamin E., 206
Chace, Elizabeth B., 155
Chasseboeuf, C. F. de, 170
Cheairs, Nathaniel F., 207
Chesnut, Mary, 207
Churchill, Winston, 15
Clark, William, 207
Clay, Clement C., 194
Clay, Henry, 59, 61
Cleburne, Patrick R., 141
Coles, Edward, 88, 94

Columbus, Christopher, 106
Combs, Bertram T., 207
Conkling, James C., 71
Coolidge, Calvin, 82
Crandall, Prudence, 120
Cranmer, Thomas, 118
Crawford, Cindy, 207
Crockett, Davy, 207
Crothers, Samuel, 94
Cruise, Tom, 207
Cyrus, Billy R., 207
Cyrus, Miley, 207
Dabney, Robert L., 54
Darwin, Charles, 176
Davis, David, 182
Davis, Jefferson, 9, 10, 16, 17, 27, 33, 40, 44, 48, 54, 56, 58, 67, 68, 74, 75, 79, 90, 162, 164-167, 172, 206, 207
Davis, Varina (Howell), 162
Day, Jeremiah, 19
Dean, Henry C., 193, 194
Dent, Frederick, 142
Dickens, Charles, 64
Dickey, James H., 94
Doak, Samuel, 94
Douglas, Stephen A., 18, 28, 52, 176, 183, 184
Douglass, Frederick, 14, 50, 188
Du Bois, William E. B., 103
Duer, William A., 19
Duvall, Robert, 207
Edward I, King, 206
Emerson, Ralph W., 50
Engels, Frederich, 21
Everett, Edward, 19, 131
Exmouth, Lord, 107
Farragut, David G., 142
Featherstonhaugh, George W., 94
Finley, Robert, 131
Foote, Shelby, 146, 206
Forbes, Christopher, 207
Forrest, Nathan B., 10, 17, 79, 133, 175, 206-208
Fox, Gustavus, 51, 53
Gadsden, Christopher, 94
Garrison, William L., 105, 129, 131, 143
Gayheart, Rebecca, 207
George III, King, 9
George, Saint, 48
Gilliland, James, 94
Gist, States R., 207
Gonzales, Antonio, 102
Goodlow, Daniel R., 132
Gordon, George W., 207, 208
Gordon, Nathaniel, 157
Gorham, Nathaniel, 30
Gracie, Archibald, 112
Grant, Jesse R., 143
Grant, Julia Boggs (Dent), 142, 143
Grant, Ulysses S., 58, 77, 79, 140, 142, 143, 167
Graves, Robert, 206
Greeley, Horace, 52, 57, 131, 143
Grey, Adeline, 190
Griffin, Cyrus, 30
Grimké, Angelina, 132
Grimké, Sarah, 132

Guaraldi, Vince, 207
Hamilton, Alexander, 27, 59, 62, 168, 169
Hamilton, J. G. de Roulhac, 178
Hamilton, James, Jr., 28
Hancock, John, 30
Hanson, John, 29
Harding, William G., 207
Hay, John, 53
Hayne, Robert Y., 88
Hedrick, Benjamin S., 132
Henderson, John, 143
Henry, Patrick, 11, 13, 94
Herndon, W. D., 171
Higginson, Thomas W., 66
Hill, Samuel, 170
Hitler, Adolf, 21, 60, 73, 82, 99, 106
Hood, John Bell, 207
Huntington, Samuel, 29, 30
Jackson, Andrew, 28, 207
Jackson, Henry R., 207
Jackson, Thomas "Stonewall", 141, 207
James II, King, 111
James, Frank, 207
James, Jesse, 207
Jamison, David F., 81
Jay, John, 27
Jefferson, Thomas, 13, 27, 35, 37, 39, 44, 48, 60, 62, 77, 80, 94, 107, 132-134, 140, 169, 207
Jent, Elias, Sr., 206
Jesus, 48, 50, 206

John, Elton, 207
Johnson, Anthony, 95
Johnson, John, 95
Johnston, Joseph E., 10, 79
Johnston, Richard M., 148
Jones, William, 142
Judd, Ashley, 207
Judd, Naomi, 207
Judd, Wynonna, 207
Jupiter (god), 73
Kautz, August V., 67
Kenner, Duncan F., 152
Kingsley, Anna, 136
Knight, Lucian I., 64
Knox, John, 118
Ladd, William, 94
Lamon, Ward H., 171
Laurens, Henry, 132
Laurens, John, 132
Lawrence, Fannie, 26
Lee, Fitzhugh, 207
Lee, Mary Anna (Custis), 140
Lee, Richard Henry, 29
Lee, Robert E., 19, 23, 50, 57, 63, 65, 77, 79, 118, 133, 140, 152, 162, 207, 208
Lee, Stephen D., 63, 64, 207
Lee, William H. F., 207
Lemen, James, 94
Lenin, Vladimir, 60
Lester, Charles E., 57
Lewis, Meriwether, 207
Limber, Jim, 162
Lincoln, Abraham, 9-11, 13, 14, 16-19, 21, 22, 26, 27, 33, 37, 39, 41, 43,

44, 46, 47, 50, 51, 53, 54, 56-60, 62, 63, 65-76, 78, 79, 83, 86, 87, 120, 121, 124, 126, 129, 131, 133, 136, 139, 140, 142, 143, 147-149, 152, 154, 155, 157, 159, 162, 164-170, 172-176, 179, 181-189, 191, 193, 194
Lincoln, Mary (Todd), 142, 171
Longstreet, James, 207
Lovejoy, Elijah P., 122
Loveless, Patty, 207
Lundy, Benjamin, 94, 132
Lyell, Charles, 87
Maclean, John, Jr., 19
Macon, Nathaniel, 94
Madison, James, 12, 27, 31, 37, 88, 94, 107, 132
Manigault, Arthur M., 207
Manigault, Joseph, 207
Marshall, James V., 35
Martineau, Harriet, 88
Marvin, Lee, 207
Marx, Karl, 21
Mason, George, 132
Maury, Abram P., 207
McCarty, Burke, 21
McGavock, Caroline E. (Winder), 207
McGavock, David H., 207
McGavock, Emily, 207
McGavock, Francis, 207
McGavock, James R., 207
McGavock, John W., 207
McGavock, Lysander, 207
McGavock, Randal W., 207
McGraw, Tim, 207
McKean, Thomas, 29
McNeil, John, 194
Meade, William, 94
Mencken, H. L., 83
Meriwether, Elizabeth A., 207
Meriwether, Minor, 207
Metoyer, Augustin, 136
Mifflin, Thomas, 29
Mills, Samuel J., 178
Monroe, James, 27
Moore, Thomas O., 66, 141
Morgan, John H., 207
Morgan, Junius, 112
Morgan, Pierpont, 112
Morton, John W., 207
Mosby, John S., 206
Mosely, Jonathan O., 89, 90
Nelson, David, 94
Nero, Claudius, 194
Nicolay, John G., 53
Nugent, Ted, 207
Obama, Barack H., 164
Oglethorpe, James E., 93
Owsley, Frank L., 80
Paine, Thomas, 170
Parton, Dolly, 207
Patrick, Saint, 48
Pellew, Edward, 107
Penn, William, 116
Peterson, Jesse L., 47
Pettus, Edmund W., 207
Phillips, Samuel, 28

Pickering, Timothy, 37
Pierce, Franklin, 28
Pillow, Gideon J., 207
Pinckney, Thomas, 28
Polk, James K., 27, 207
Polk, Leonidas, 207
Polk, Lucius E., 207
Pollard, Edward A., 53, 54, 126
Pomeroy, Samuel C., 179
Presley, Elvis, 207
Quamina, King, 108
Randolph, Edmund J., 207
Randolph, George W., 207
Rankin, John, 94
Rawle, William, 40
Reagan, Ronald, 207
Reynolds, Burt, 207
Rhodes, James R., 175
Richardson, John A., 65
Riley, Benjamin F., 158
Robbins, Hargus, 207
Robert the Bruce, King, 206
Rowland, David S., 31
Rucker, Edmund W., 207
Rutgers, Henry, 19, 131
Scott, Winfield, 52, 142
Scruggs, Earl, 207
Seabrook, John L., 207
Seabrook, Lochlainn, 11-13, 206, 207, 209
Seger, Bob, 207
Seneca, the Younger, 194
Sewall, Samuel, 112
Seward, William H., 46, 74, 185
Sheridan, Philip, 194
Sherman, William T., 194
Shields, James A., 172
Shufeldt, Robert W., 175
Simon, John Y., 182
Skaggs, Ricky, 207
Smith, Caleb B., 52
Smith, Robert, 31
Sori, Abdul Rahman Ibrahim Ibn, 61
Sparks, Jared, 121, 131
Spooner, Lysander, 86
St. Clair, Arthur, 30
Stalin, Joseph, 60, 73, 99, 106
Stanton, Edwin M., 78
Stephens, Alexander H., 9, 10, 33, 34, 57, 62, 147, 148, 183, 206
Stevens, Thaddeus, 175
Stewart, Alexander P., 207
Still, William, 149
Stonebraker, J. Clarence, 161
Stowe, Harriet B., 26, 131
Strachan, William, 194
Strain, Tara, 208
Strain, Thomas V., Jr., 13, 208
Stuart, Jeb, 207
Stuart, John T., 170
Sturge, Joseph, 88
Suetonius, 194
Sumner, Charles, 57, 101
Sweet, Benjamin J., 78
Tabor, George R., 208
Taylor, Richard, 10, 207
Taylor, Sarah K., 207
Taylor, Zachary, 207
Thomas, George H., 142
Thome, James A., 94

Thoreau, Henry D., 50
Tiffany, Charles, 112
Tocqueville, Alexis de, 31, 32, 42, 77, 87
Toombs, Robert A., 27
Trumbull, Lyman, 185
Tucker, St. George, 77, 94
Turchin, John B., 194
Tynes, Ellen B., 207
Van Buren, Martin, 27
Vance, Robert B., 207
Vance, Zebulon, 207
Venable, Charles S., 207
Volney, Count, 170
Voltaire, 170
Wakefield, John A., 172
Washington, Booker T., 139
Washington, George, 9, 13, 28-30, 44, 94, 118, 132, 140, 193
Washington, John A., 207
Washington, Thornton A., 207
Welles, Gideon, 51, 53
Wesley, Charles H., 179
Wesley, John, 118
White, Henry A., 118
Wilson, Woodrow, 185, 207
Winder, Charles S., 207
Winder, John H., 207
Witherspoon, Reese, 207
Womack, John B., 207
Womack, Lee Ann, 207
Zeus (god), 73
Zollicoffer, Felix K., 207

MEET THE AUTHOR

LOCHLAINN SEABROOK, winner of the prestigious Jefferson Davis Historical Gold Medal for his "masterpiece," *A Rebel Born: A Defense of Nathan Bedford Forrest*, is an unreconstructed Southern historian, award-winning author, Civil War scholar, and traditional Southern Agrarian of Scottish, English, Irish, Dutch, Welsh, German, and Italian extraction. An encyclopedist, lexicographer, musician, artist, graphic designer, genealogist, and photographer, as well as an award-winning poet, songwriter, and screenwriter, he has a 40 year background in historical nonfiction writing and is a member of the Sons of Confederate Veterans, the Civil War Trust, and the National Grange.

Due to similarities in their writing styles, ideas, and literary works, Seabrook is often referred to as the "new Shelby Foote," the "Southern Joseph Campbell," and the "American Robert Graves" (his English cousin).

The grandson of an Appalachian coal-mining family, Seabrook is a seventh-generation Kentuckian, co-chair of the Jent/Gent Family Committee (Kentucky), founder and director of the Blakeney Family Tree Project, and a board member of the Friends of Colonel Benjamin E. Caudill. Seabrook's literary works have been endorsed by leading authorities, museum curators, award-winning historians, bestselling authors, celebrities, noted scientists, well respected educators, TV show hosts and producers, renowned military artists, esteemed Southern organizations, and distinguished academicians from around the world.

Seabrook has authored over 45 popular adult books on the American Civil War, American and international slavery, the U.S. Confederacy (1781), the Southern Confederacy (1861), religion, theology and thealogy, Jesus, the Bible, the Apocrypha, the Law of Attraction, alternative health, spirituality, ghost stories, the paranormal, ufology, social issues, and cross-cultural studies of the family and marriage. His Confederate biographies, pro-South studies, genealogical monographs, family histories, military encyclopedias, self-help guides, and etymological dictionaries have received wide acclaim.

Seabrook's eight children's books include a Southern guide to the Civil War, a biography of Nathan Bedford Forrest, a dictionary of religion and myth, a rewriting of the King Arthur legend (which reinstates the original pre-Christian motifs), two bedtime stories for preschoolers, a naturalist's guidebook to owls, a worldwide look at the family, and an examination of the Near-Death Experience.

Of blue-blooded Southern stock through his Kentucky, Tennessee, Virginia, West Virginia, and North Carolina ancestors, he is a direct descendant of European royalty via his 6th great-grandfather, the Earl of Oxford, after which London's famous Harley Street is named. Among his celebrated male Celtic ancestors is Robert the Bruce, King of Scotland, Seabrook's 22nd great-grandfather. The 21st great-grandson of Edward I "Longshanks" Plantagenet), King of England, Seabrook is a thirteenth-generation Southerner through his descent from the colonists of Jamestown, Virginia (1607).

The 2nd, 3rd, and 4th great-grandson of dozens of Confederate soldiers, one of his closest connections to Lincoln's War is through his 3rd great-grandfather, Elias Jent, Sr., who fought for the Confederacy in the Thirteenth Cavalry Kentucky under Seabrook's 2nd cousin, Colonel Benjamin E. Caudill. The Thirteenth, also known as "Caudill's Army," fought in numerous conflicts, including the Battles of Saltville, Gladsville, Mill Cliff, Poor Fork, Whitesburg, and Leatherwood.

Seabrook is a descendant of the families of Alexander H. Stephens, John Singleton Mosby,

Lochlainn Seabrook, award-winning Civil War scholar & unreconstructed Southern historian.

William Giles Harding, and Edmund Winchester Rucker, and is related to the following Confederates and other 19th-Century luminaries: Robert E. Lee, Stephen Dill Lee, Stonewall Jackson, Nathan Bedford Forrest, James Longstreet, John Hunt Morgan, Jeb Stuart, Pierre G. T. Beauregard (approved the Confederate Battle Flag design), George W. Gordon, John Bell Hood, Alexander Peter Stewart, Arthur M. Manigault, Joseph Manigault, Charles Scott Venable, Thornton A. Washington, John A. Washington, Abraham Buford, Edmund W. Pettus, Theodrick "Tod" Carter, John B. Womack, John H. Winder, Gideon J. Pillow, States Rights Gist, Henry R. Jackson, John Lawton Seabrook, John C. Breckinridge, Leonidas Polk, Zachary Taylor, Sarah Knox Taylor (first wife of Jefferson Davis), Richard Taylor, Davy Crockett, Daniel Boone, Meriwether Lewis (of the Lewis and Clark Expedition) Andrew Jackson, James K. Polk, Abram Poindexter Maury (founder of Franklin, TN), Zebulon Vance, Thomas Jefferson, Edmund Jennings Randolph, George Wythe Randolph (grandson of Jefferson), Felix K. Zollicoffer, Fitzhugh Lee, Nathaniel F. Cheairs, Jesse James, Frank James, Robert Brank Vance, Charles Sidney Winder, John W. McGavock, Caroline E. (Winder) McGavock, David Harding McGavock, Lysander McGavock, James Randal McGavock, Randal William McGavock, Francis McGavock, Emily McGavock, William Henry F. Lee, Lucius E. Polk, Minor Meriwether (husband of noted pro-South author Elizabeth Avery Meriwether), Ellen Bourne Tynes (wife of Forrest's chief of artillery, Captain John W. Morton), South Carolina Senators Preston Smith Brooks and Andrew Pickens Butler, and famed South Carolina diarist Mary Chesnut.

(Photo © Lochlainn Seabrook)

Seabrook's modern day cousins include: Patrick J. Buchanan (conservative author), Cindy Crawford (model), Shelby Lee Adams (Letcher Co., Kentucky, photographer), Bertram Thomas Combs (Kentucky's 50th governor), Edith Bolling (wife of President Woodrow Wilson), and actors Robert Duvall, Reese Witherspoon, Lee Marvin, Rebecca Gayheart, Andy Griffith, and Tom Cruise.

Seabrook's screenplay, *A Rebel Born*, based on his book of the same name, has been signed with acclaimed filmmaker Christopher Forbes (of Forbes Film). It is now in pre-production, and is set for release in 2016 as a full-length feature film. This will be the first movie ever made of Nathan Bedford Forrest's life story, and as a historically accurate project written from the Southern perspective, is destined to be one of the most talked about Civil War films of all time.

Born with music in his blood, Seabrook is an award-winning, multi-genre, BMI-Nashville songwriter and lyricist who has composed some 3,000 songs (250 albums), and whose original music has been heard in film (*A Rebel Born, Cowgirls 'n Angels, Confederate Cavalry, Billy the Kid: Showdown in Lincoln County, Vengeance Without Mercy, Last Step, County Line, The Mark*) and on TV and radio worldwide. A musician, producer, multi-instrumentalist, and renown performer—whose keyboard work has been variously compared to pianists from Hargus Robbins and Vince Guaraldi to Elton John and Leonard Bernstein—Seabrook has opened for groups such as the Earl Scruggs Review, Ted Nugent, and Bob Seger, and has performed privately for such public figures as President Ronald Reagan, Burt Reynolds, Loni Anderson, and Senator Edward W. Brooke. Seabrook's cousins in the music business include: Johnny Cash, Elvis Presley, Billy Ray and Miley Cyrus, Patty Loveless, Tim McGraw, Lee Ann Womack, Dolly Parton, Pat Boone, Naomi, Wynonna, and Ashley Judd, Ricky Skaggs, the Sunshine Sisters, Martha Carson, and Chet Atkins.

Seabrook, a libertarian, lives with his wife and family in historic Middle Tennessee, the heart of Forrest country and the Confederacy, where his conservative Southern ancestors fought valiantly against Liberal Lincoln and the progressive North in defense of Jeffersonianism, constitutional government, and personal liberty.

LochlainnSeabrook.com

MEET THE FOREWORD WRITER

THOMAS V. STRAIN JR., current Lt. Commander-in-Chief of the Sons of Confederate Veterans, is a veteran of Operation Desert Storm and a descendant of famed Confederate General George W. Gordon, Eleventh Tennessee Cavalry.

The winner of numerous Confederate awards and accommodations, including the Robert E. Lee Medal, he is a member of the Forrest Boyhood Home, a five-time recipient of the SCV's Meritorious Service Medal, and a three-time recipient of the Distinguished Service Medal.

From 2006 to 2008 he served as the SCV's Deputy Chief of Staff, and in 2007 and 2009 he was the winner of both the Dr. George R. Tabor Distinguished Camp of the Year and the Dr. James B. Butler Historical Project of the Year. In 2006, 2007, and 2010, he won the Alabama Division Camp of the Year and Newsletter of the Year.

Strain, who owns Heart of Dixie Lawn and Landscape, lives with his wife Tara in Alabama and is a lifetime member of the SCV and the Alabama Division, the latter of which he was commander in 2012.

SCV.org

Lochlainn Seabrook ∞ 209

If you enjoyed this book you will be interested in Mr. Seabrook's other popular Civil War related titles:

- Everything You Were Taught About the Civil War is Wrong, Ask a Southerner!
- Everything You Were Taught About American Slavery is Wrong, Ask a Southerner!
- Give This Book to a Yankee! A Southern Guide to the Civil War for Northerners
- Confederacy 101: Amazing Facts You Never Knew About America's Oldest Political Tradition

Available from Sea Raven Press and wherever fine books are sold

ALL OF OUR BOOK COVERS ARE AVAILABLE AS 11" X 17" POSTERS, SUITABLE FOR FRAMING.

SeaRavenPress.com

www.ingramcontent.com/pod-product-compliance
Lightning Source LLC
Chambersburg PA
CBHW032112090426
42743CB00007B/323